The Law School Admission Council (LSAC) is a nonprofit corporation whose members are more than 200 law schools, 15 of which are in Canada; the rest are in the United States. It was founded in 1947 to coordinate, facilitate, and enhance the law school admission process. The organization also provides programs and services related to legal education. All law schools approved by the American Bar Association (ABA) are LSAC members. Canadian law schools recognized by a provincial or territorial law society or government agency are also included in the voting membership of the Council.

The services provided by LSAC include the Law School Admission Test (LSAT); the Law School Data Assembly Service (LSDAS); the Candidate Referral Service (CRS); software including Admit-M admission office software and electronic law school applications on the web and CD-ROM; and various publications and LSAT preparation tools. The LSAT, the LSDAS, and CRS are provided to assist law schools in serving and evaluating applicants. LSAC does not engage in assessing an applicant's chances for admission to any law school; all admission decisions are made by individual law schools.

LSAT; *The Official LSAT PrepTest; LSAT: The Official TriplePrep; Admit-M;* and LSAC are registered marks of the Law School Admission Council, Inc. Law School Forums is a service mark of the Law School Admission Council, Inc. *LSAT: The Official TriplePrep Plus; The Official LSAT PrepTest with Explanations; The Official LSAT SuperPrep; 10 Actual, Official LSAT PrepTests; 10 More Actual, Official LSAT PrepTests; The Next 10 Actual, Official LSAT PrepTests; The New Whole Law School Package; ABA-LSAC Official Guide to ABA-Approved Law Schools; LSACD;* and LSDAS are trademarks of Law School Admission Council, Inc.

Law School Admission Council fees, policies, and procedures relating to, but not limited to, test registration, test administration, test score reporting, misconduct and irregularities, and other matters may change without notice at any time. Up-to-date Law School Admission Council policies and procedures are available at *www.LSAC.org* and in the *Registration and Information Book,* or you may contact our candidate service representatives.

ISBN 0-942639-95-2

Table of Contents

The Law School Admission Test is a half-day standardized test required for admission to all LSAC-member law schools. It consists of five 35-minute sections of multiple-choice questions. Four of the five sections contribute to the test taker's score. These sections include one reading comprehension section, one analytical reasoning section, and two logical reasoning sections. The unscored section typically is used to pretest new test items and to preequate new test forms. The placement of this section, which is commonly referred to as the variable section, is varied for each administration of the test. A 30-minute writing sample is administered at the end of the test. The writing sample is not scored by LSAC, but copies are sent to all law schools to which you apply. The score scale for the LSAT is 120 to 180.

The LSAT is designed to measure skills that are considered essential for success in law school: the reading and comprehension of complex texts with accuracy and insight; the organization and management of information and the ability to draw reasonable inferences from it; the ability to think critically; and the analysis and evaluation of the reasoning and arguments of others.

The LSAT provides a standard measure of acquired reading and verbal reasoning skills that law schools can use as one of several factors in assessing applicants.

For up-to-date information about LSAC's services, go to our website, *www.LSAC.org* or pick up a current *LSAT & LSDAS Registration and Information Book*.

Scoring

Your LSAT score is based on the number of questions you answer correctly (the raw score). There is no deduction for incorrect answers, and all questions count equally. In other words, there is no penalty for guessing.

■ Test Score Accuracy—Reliability and Standard Error of Measurement

Candidates perform at different levels on different occasions for reasons quite unrelated to the characteristics of a test itself. The accuracy of test scores is best described by the use of two related statistical terms: reliability and standard error of measurement.

Reliability is a measure of how consistently a test measures the skills being assessed. The higher the reliability coefficient for a test, the more certain we can be that test takers would get very similar scores if they took the test again.

LSAC reports an internal consistency measure of reliability for every test form. Reliability can vary from 0.00 to 1.00, and a test with no measurement error would have a reliability coefficient of 1.00 (never attained in practice). Reliability coefficients for past LSAT forms have ranged from .90 to .95, indicating a high degree of consistency for these tests. LSAC expects the reliability of the LSAT to continue to fall within the same range.

LSAC also reports the amount of measurement error associated with each test form, a concept known as the standard error of measurement (SEM). The SEM, which is usually about 2.6 points, indicates how close a test taker's observed score is likely to be to his or her true score. True scores are theoretical scores that would be obtained from perfectly reliable tests with no measurement error—scores never known in practice.

Score bands, or ranges of scores that contain a test taker's true score a certain percentage of the time, can be derived using the SEM. LSAT score bands are constructed by adding and subtracting the (rounded) SEM to and from an actual LSAT score (e.g., the LSAT score, plus or minus 3 points). Scores near 120 or 180 have asymmetrical bands. Score bands constructed in this manner will contain an individual's true score approximately 68 percent of the time.

Measurement error also must be taken into account when comparing LSAT scores of two test takers. It is likely that small differences in scores are due to measurement error rather than to meaningful differences in ability. The standard error of score differences provides some guidance as to the importance of differences between two scores. The standard error of score differences is approximately 1.4 times larger than the standard error of measurement for the individual scores.

Thus, a test score should be regarded as a useful but approximate measure of a test taker's abilities as measured by the test, not as an exact determination of his or her abilities. LSAC encourages law schools to examine the range of scores within the interval that probably contains the test taker's true score (e.g., the test taker's score band) rather than solely interpret the reported score alone.

Adjustments for Variation in Test Difficulty

All test forms of the LSAT reported on the same score scale are designed to measure the same abilities, but one test form may be slightly easier or more difficult than another. The scores from different test forms are made comparable through a statistical procedure known as equating. As a result of equating, a given scaled score earned on different test forms reflects the same level of ability.

Research on the LSAT

Summaries of LSAT validity studies and other LSAT research can be found in member law school libraries.

To Inquire About Test Questions

If you find what you believe to be an error or ambiguity in a test question that affects your response to the question, contact LSAC by e-mail: *LSATTS@LSAC.org*, or write to Law School Admission Council, Test Development Group, Box 40, Newtown, PA 18940-0040.

How This PrepTest Differs from an Actual LSAT

This PrepTest is made up of the scored sections and writing sample from the actual disclosed LSAT administered in October 2004. However, it does not contain the extra, variable section that is used to pretest new test items of one of the three question types. The three LSAT question types may be in a different order in an actual LSAT than in this PrepTest. This is because the order of the question types is intentionally varied for each administration of the test.

The Question Types

The multiple-choice questions that make up most of the LSAT reflect a broad range of academic disciplines and are intended to give no advantage to candidates from a particular academic background.

The five sections of the test contain three different question types. The following material presents a general discussion of the nature of each question type and some strategies that can be used in answering them.

Reading Comprehension Questions

The purpose of reading comprehension questions is to measure your ability to read, with understanding and insight, examples of lengthy and complex materials similar to those commonly encountered in law school work. The reading comprehension section of the test consists of four passages, each approximately 450 words long, followed by five to eight questions that test your reading and reasoning abilities. Passages for reading comprehension items are drawn from subjects such as the humanities, the social sciences, the biological and physical sciences, and issues related to the law.

Reading comprehension questions require you to read carefully and accurately, to determine the relationships among the various parts of the passage, and to draw reasonable inferences from the material in the passage. The questions may ask about:

- the main idea or primary purpose of the passage;

- the meaning or purpose of words or phrases used in the passage;

- information explicitly stated in the passage;

- information or ideas that can be inferred from the passage;

- the organization of the passage;

- the application of information in the passage to a new context; and

- the tone of the passage or the author's attitude as it is revealed in the language used.

Suggested Approach

Since passages are drawn from many different disciplines and sources, you should not be discouraged if you encounter material with which you are not familiar. It is important to remember that questions are to be answered exclusively on the basis of the information provided in the passage. There is no particular knowledge that you are expected to bring to the test, and you should not make inferences based on any prior knowledge of a subject that you may have. You may, however, wish to defer working on a passage that seems particularly difficult or unfamiliar until after you have dealt with passages you find easier.

Strategies. In preparing for the test, you should experiment with different strategies, and decide which work most effectively for you. These include:

- Reading the passage very closely and then answering the questions;

- Reading the questions first, reading the passage closely, and then returning to the questions; and

- Skimming the passage and questions very quickly, then rereading the passage closely and answering the questions.

Remember that your strategy must be effective under timed conditions.

Reading the passage. Whatever strategy you choose, you should give the passage at least one careful reading before answering the questions. Separate main ideas from supporting ideas and the author's own ideas or attitudes from factual, objective information. Note transitions from one idea to the next and examine the relationships among the different ideas or parts of the passage. For example, are they contrasting or complementary? Consider how and why the author makes points and draws conclusions. Be sensitive to the implications of what the passage says.

You may find it helpful to mark key parts of the passage. For example, you might underline main ideas or important arguments, and you might circle transitional words—'although,' 'nevertheless,' 'correspondingly,' and the like—that will help you map the structure of the passage. Moreover, you might note descriptive words that will help you identify the author's attitude toward a particular idea or person.

Answering the Questions

- Always read all the answer choices before selecting the best answer. The best answer choice is the one that most accurately and completely answers the question being posed.

- Respond to the specific question being asked. Do not pick an answer choice simply because it is a true statement. For example, picking a true statement might yield an incorrect answer to a question in which you are asked to identify the author's position on an issue, since here you are not being asked to evaluate the truth of the author's position, but only to correctly identify what that position is.

- Answer the questions only on the basis of the information provided in the passage. Your own views, interpretations, or opinions, and those you have heard from others, may sometimes conflict with those expressed in the passage; however, you are expected to work within the context provided by the passage. You should not expect to agree with everything you encounter in reading comprehension passages.

■ Analytical Reasoning Questions

Analytical reasoning items are designed to measure your ability to understand a structure of relationships and to draw logical conclusions about the structure. You are asked to make deductions from a set of statements, rules, or conditions that describe relationships among entities such as persons, places, things, or events. They simulate the kinds of detailed analyses of relationships that a law student must perform in solving legal problems. For example, a passage might describe four diplomats sitting around a table, following certain rules of protocol as to who can sit where. You must answer questions about the implications of the given information, for example, who is sitting between diplomats X and Y.

The passage used for each group of questions describes a common relationship such as the following:

- Assignment: Two parents, P and O, and their children, R and S, must go to the dentist on four consecutive days, designated 1, 2, 3, and 4;

- Ordering: X arrived before Y but after Z;

- Grouping: A manager is trying to form a project team from seven staff members—R,S,T,U,V,W, and X. Each staff member has a particular strength—writing, planning, or facilitating;

- Spatial: A certain country contains six cities and each city is connected to at least one other city by a system of roads, some of which are one-way.

Careful reading and analysis are necessary to determine the exact nature of the relationships involved. Some relationships are fixed (e.g., P and R always sit at the same table). Other relationships are variable (e.g., Q must be assigned to either table 1 or table 3). Some relationships that are not stated in the conditions are implied by and can be deduced from those that are stated. (e.g., If one condition about books on a shelf specifies that Book L is to the left of Book Y, and another specifies that Book P is to the left of Book L, then it can be deduced that Book P is to the left of Book Y.)

No formal training in logic is required to answer these questions correctly. Analytical reasoning questions are intended to be answered using knowledge, skills, and reasoning ability generally expected of college students and graduates.

Suggested Approach

Some people may prefer to answer first those questions about a passage that seem less difficult and then those that seem more difficult. In general, it is best not to start another passage before finishing one begun earlier, because much time can be lost in returning to a passage and reestablishing familiarity with its relationships. Do not assume that, because the conditions for a set of questions look long or complicated, the questions based on those conditions will necessarily be especially difficult.

Reading the passage. In reading the conditions, do not introduce unwarranted assumptions. For instance, in a set establishing relationships of height and weight among the members of a team, do not assume that a person who is taller than another person must weigh more than that person. All the information needed to answer each question is provided in the passage and the question itself.

The conditions are designed to be as clear as possible; do not interpret them as if they were intended to trick you. For example, if a question asks how many people could be eligible to serve on a committee, consider only those people named in the passage unless directed otherwise. When in doubt, read the conditions in their most obvious sense. Remember, however, that the language in the conditions is intended to be read for precise meaning. It is essential to pay particular attention to words that describe or limit relationships, such as 'only,' 'exactly,' 'never,' 'always,' 'must be,' 'cannot be,' and the like.

The result of this careful reading will be a clear picture of the structure of the relationships involved, including the kinds of relationships permitted, the participants in the relationships, and the range of actions or attributes allowed by the relationships for these participants.

Questions are independent. Each question should be considered separately from the other questions in its set; no information, except what is given in the original conditions, should be carried over from one question to another. In some cases a question will simply ask for conclusions to be drawn from the conditions as originally given. Some questions may, however, add information to the original conditions or temporarily suspend one of the original conditions for the purpose of that question only. For example, if Question 1 adds the information "if P is sitting at table 2...," this information should NOT be carried over to any other question in the group.

Highlighting the text; using diagrams. Many people find it useful to underline key points in the passage and in each question. In addition, it may prove very helpful to draw a diagram to assist you in finding the solution to the problem.

In preparing for the test, you may wish to experiment with different types of diagrams. For a scheduling problem, a calendar-like diagram may be helpful. For a spatial relationship problem, a simple map can be a useful device.

Even though some people find diagrams to be very helpful, other people seldom use them. And among those who do regularly use diagrams in solving these problems, there is by no means universal agreement on which kind of diagram is best for which problem or in which cases a diagram is most useful. Do not be concerned if a particular problem in the test seems to be best approached without the use of a diagram.

■ Logical Reasoning Questions

Logical reasoning questions evaluate your ability to understand, analyze, criticize, and complete a variety of arguments. The arguments are contained in short passages taken from a variety of sources, including letters to the editor, speeches, advertisements, newspaper articles and editorials, informal discussions and conversations, as well as articles in the humanities, the social sciences, and the natural sciences.

Each logical reasoning question requires you to read and comprehend a short passage, then answer one or two questions about it. The questions test a variety of abilities involved in reasoning logically and thinking critically. These include:

- recognizing the point or issue of an argument or dispute;

- detecting the assumptions involved in an argumentation or chain of reasoning;

- drawing reasonable conclusions from given evidence or premises;

- identifying and applying principles;

- identifying the method or structure of an argument or chain of reasoning;

- detecting reasoning errors and misinterpretations;

- determining how additional evidence or argumentation affects an argument or conclusion; and

- identifying explanations and recognizing resolutions of conflicting facts or arguments.

The questions do not presuppose knowledge of the terminology of formal logic. For example, you will not be expected to know the meaning of specialized terms such as "ad hominem" or "syllogism." On the other hand, you will be expected to understand and critique the reasoning contained in arguments. This requires that you possess, at a minimum, a college-level understanding of widely used concepts such as argument, premise, assumption, and conclusion.

Suggested Approach

Read each question carefully. Make sure that you understand the meaning of each part of the question. Make sure that you understand the meaning of each answer choice and the ways in which it may or may not relate to the question posed.

Do not pick a response simply because it is a true statement. Although true, it may not answer the question posed.

Answer each question on the basis of the information that is given, even if you do not agree with it. Work within the context provided by the passage. LSAT questions do not involve any tricks or hidden meanings.

The Writing Exercise

Test takers are given 30 minutes to complete the brief writing exercise, which is not scored but is used by law school admission personnel to assess writing skill. Read the topic carefully. You will probably find it best to spend a few minutes considering the topic and organizing your thoughts before you begin writing. **Do not write on a topic other than the one specified. Writing on a topic of your own choice is not acceptable.**

There is no "right" or "wrong" position on the writing sample topic. Law schools are interested in how skillfully you support the position you take and how clearly you express that position. How well you write is much more important than how much you write. No special knowledge is required or expected. Law schools are interested in organization, vocabulary, and writing mechanics. They understand the short time available to you and the pressure under which you are writing.

Confine your writing to the lined area following the writing sample topic. You will find that you have enough space if you plan your writing carefully, write on every line, avoid wide margins, and keep your handwriting a reasonable size. Be sure that your handwriting is legible.

Scratch paper is provided for use during the writing sample portion of the test only. Scratch paper cannot be used in other sections of the LSAT.

The writing sample is photocopied and sent to law schools to which you direct your LSAT score.

Some writing sample prompts, or variations of them, may be given at more than one LSAT administration. A collection of 50 representative writing prompts is included in *LSAT: The Official TriplePrep Plus*, published by LSAC.

Taking the PrepTest Under Simulated LSAT Conditions

One important way to prepare for the LSAT is to simulate the day of the test by taking a practice test under actual time constraints. Taking a practice test under timed conditions helps you to estimate the amount of time you can afford to spend on each question in a section and to determine the question types on which you may need additional practice.

Since the LSAT is a timed test, it is important to use your allotted time wisely. During the test, you may work only on the section designated by the test supervisor. You cannot devote extra time to a difficult section and make up that time on a section you find easier. In pacing yourself, and checking your answers, you should think of each section of the test as a separate minitest.

Be sure that you answer every question on the test. When you do not know the correct answer to a question, first eliminate the responses that you know are incorrect, then make your best guess among the remaining choices. Do not be afraid to guess as there is no penalty for incorrect answers.

When you take a sample test abide by all the requirements specified in the directions and keep strictly within the specified time limits. Work without a rest period. When you take an actual test you will have only a short break—usually 10-15 minutes—after SECTION III. When taken under conditions as much like actual testing conditions as possible, a sample test provides very useful preparation for taking the LSAT.

Official directions are included in this PrepTest so that you can approximate actual testing conditions as you practice.

To take the test:

- Set a timer for 35 minutes. Answer all the questions in SECTION I of this PrepTest. Stop working on that section when the 35 minutes have elapsed.

- Repeat, allowing yourself 35 minutes each for sections II, III, and IV.

- Set the timer for 30 minutes, then prepare your response to the writing sample for the PrepTest.

- Refer to "Computing Your Score" for the PrepTest for instruction on evaluating your performance. An answer key is provided for that purpose.

The sample test that follows consists of four sections corresponding to the four scored sections of the October 2004 LSAT.

General Directions for the LSAT Answer Sheet

The actual testing time for this portion of the test will be 2 hours 55 minutes. There are five sections, each with a time limit of 35 minutes. The supervisor will tell you when to begin and end each section. If you finish a section before time is called, you may check your work on that section <u>only</u>; do not turn to any other section of the test book and do not work on any other section either in the test book or on the answer sheet.

There are several different types of questions on the test, and each question type has its own directions. <u>Be sure you understand the directions for each question type before attempting to answer any questions in that section.</u>

Not everyone will finish all the questions in the time allowed. Do not hurry, but work steadily and as quickly as you can without sacrificing accuracy. You are advised to use your time effectively. If a question seems too difficult, go on to the next one and return to the difficult question after completing the section. MARK THE BEST ANSWER YOU CAN FOR EVERY QUESTION. NO DEDUCTIONS WILL BE MADE FOR WRONG ANSWERS. YOUR SCORE WILL BE BASED ONLY ON THE NUMBER OF QUESTIONS YOU ANSWER CORRECTLY.

ALL YOUR ANSWERS MUST BE MARKED ON THE ANSWER SHEET. Answer spaces for each question are lettered to correspond with the letters of the potential answers to each question in the test book. After you have decided which of the answers is correct, blacken the corresponding space on the answer sheet. BE SURE THAT EACH MARK IS BLACK AND COMPLETELY FILLS THE ANSWER SPACE. Give only one answer to each question. If you change an answer, be sure that all previous marks are <u>erased completely</u>. Since the answer sheet is machine scored, incomplete erasures may be interpreted as intended answers. ANSWERS RECORDED IN THE TEST BOOK WILL NOT BE SCORED.

There may be more questions noted on this answer sheet than there are questions in a section. Do not be concerned but be certain that the section and number of the question you are answering matches the answer sheet section and question number. Additional answer spaces in any answer sheet section should be left blank. Begin your next section in the number one answer space for that section.

LSAC takes various steps to ensure that answer sheets are returned from test centers in a timely manner for processing. In the unlikely event that an answer sheet(s) is not received, LSAC will permit the examinee to either retest at no additional fee or to receive a refund of his or her LSAT fee. THESE REMEDIES ARE THE EXCLUSIVE REMEDIES AVAILABLE IN THE UNLIKELY EVENT THAT AN ANSWER SHEET IS NOT RECEIVED BY LSAC.

Score Cancellation

Complete this section only if you are absolutely certain you want to cancel your score. A CANCELLATION REQUEST CANNOT BE RESCINDED. IF YOU ARE AT ALL UNCERTAIN, YOU SHOULD NOT COMPLETE THIS SECTION; INSTEAD, YOU SHOULD CONSIDER SUBMITTING A SIGNED SCORE CANCELLATION FORM, WHICH MUST BE RECEIVED AT LSAC WITHIN 9 CALENDAR DAYS OF THE TEST.

To cancel your score from this administration, you **must:**

A. fill in both ovals here ..... ◯◯

AND

B. read the following statement. Then sign your name and enter the date.
YOUR SIGNATURE ALONE IS NOT SUFFICIENT FOR SCORE CANCELLATION. BOTH OVALS ABOVE MUST BE FILLED IN FOR SCANNING EQUIPMENT TO RECOGNIZE YOUR REQUEST FOR SCORE CANCELLATION.

I certify that I wish to cancel my test score from this administration. I understand that my request is irreversible and that my score will not be sent to me or to the law schools to which I apply.

_____
Sign your name in full

_____
Date

HOW DID YOU PREPARE FOR THE LSAT?
(Select all that apply.)

Responses to this item are voluntary and will be used for statistical research purposes only.

◯ By studying the sample questions in the *LSAT Registration and Information Book.*
◯ By taking the free sample LSAT in the *LSAT Registration and Information Book.*
◯ By working through *The Official LSAT Prep Test(s) and/or TriplePrep.*
◯ By using a book on how to prepare for the LSAT not published by LSAC.
◯ By attending a commercial test preparation or coaching course.
◯ By attending a test preparation or coaching course offered through an undergraduate institution.
◯ Self study.
◯ Other preparation.
◯ No preparation.

CERTIFYING STATEMENT

Please write (DO NOT PRINT) the following statement. Sign and date.

I certify that I am the examinee whose name appears on this answer sheet and that I am here to take the LSAT for the sole purpose of being considered for admission to law school. I further certify that I will neither assist nor receive assistance from any other candidate, and I agree not to copy or retain examination questions or to transmit them in any form to any other person.

_____
_____
_____
_____
_____
_____
_____
_____

SIGNATURE: _____   TODAY'S DATE: ___/___/___
                                                                          MONTH DAY YEAR

INSTRUCTIONS FOR COMPLETING THE BIOGRAPHICAL AREA ARE ON THE BACK COVER OF YOUR TEST BOOKLET.
USE ONLY A NO. 2 OR HB PENCIL TO COMPLETE THIS ANSWER SHEET. DO NOT USE INK.

A

USE A NO. 2 PENCIL ONLY   ● Right Mark   ⊘ ⊗ ⊙ Wrong Marks

1 LAST NAME   FIRST NAME   MI

2 SOCIAL SECURITY/ SOCIAL INSURANCE NO.

3 LSAC ACCOUNT NUMBER   L

4 DATE OF BIRTH

MONTH	DAY	YEAR
Jan		
Feb		
Mar		
Apr		
May		
June		
July		
Aug		
Sept		
Oct		
Nov		
Dec		

5 RACIAL/ETHNIC DESCRIPTION

- 1 American Indian/ Alaskan Native
- 2 Asian/Pacific Islander
- 3 Black/African Amer.
- 4 Canadian Aboriginal
- 5 Caucasian/White
- 6 Chicano/Mex. Amer.
- 7 Hispanic/Latino
- 8 Puerto Rican
- 9 Other

6 GENDER
- Male
- Female

7 DOMINANT LANGUAGE
- English
- Other

8 ENGLISH FLUENCY
- Yes   No

9 TEST BOOK SERIAL NO.

10 TEST FORM

11 TEST DATE
MONTH   DAY   YEAR

12 CENTER NUMBER

13 TEST FORM CODE

Law School Admission Test

Mark one and only one answer to each question. Be sure to fill in completely the space for your intended answer choice. If you erase, do so completely. Make no stray marks.

SECTION 1 / SECTION 2 / SECTION 3 / SECTION 4 / SECTION 5

Questions 1–30, each with answer choices A B C D E.

14 PLEASE PRINT ALL INFORMATION

LAST NAME   FIRST

SOCIAL SECURITY/SOCIAL INSURANCE NO.

DATE OF BIRTH

MAILING ADDRESS

NOTE: If you have a new address you must write LSAC at Box 2000-C, Newtown, PA 18940 or call (215) 968-1001.

FOR LSAC USE ONLY

LR	LW	LCS

● Ⓐ Ⓑ Ⓒ Ⓓ

SECTION I

Time—35 minutes

27 Questions

Directions: Each passage in this section is followed by a group of questions to be answered on the basis of what is <u>stated</u> or <u>implied</u> in the passage. For some of the questions, more than one of the choices could conceivably answer the question. However, you are to choose the <u>best</u> answer; that is, the response that most accurately and completely answers the question, and blacken the corresponding space on your answer sheet.

The Canadian Auto Workers' (CAW) Legal Services Plan, designed to give active and retired autoworkers and their families access to totally prepaid or partially reimbursed legal services, has
(5) been in operation since late 1985. Plan members have the option of using either the plan's staff lawyers, whose services are fully covered by the cost of membership in the plan, or an outside lawyer. Outside lawyers, in turn, can either sign up with the plan as a
(10) "cooperating lawyer" and accept the CAW's fee schedule as payment in full, or they can charge a higher fee and collect the balance from the client. Autoworkers appear to have embraced the notion of prepaid legal services: 45 percent of eligible union
(15) members were enrolled in the plan by 1988. Moreover, the idea of prepaid legal services has been spreading in Canada. A department store is even offering a plan to holders of its credit card.

While many plan members seem to be happy to
(20) get reduced-cost legal help, many lawyers are concerned about the plan's effect on their profession, especially its impact on prices for legal services. Some point out that even though most lawyers have not joined the plan as cooperating lawyers, legal fees
(25) in the cities in which the CAW plan operates have been depressed, in some cases to an unprofitable level. The directors of the plan, however, claim that both clients and lawyers benefit from their arrangement. For while the clients get ready access to
(30) reduced-price services, lawyers get professional contact with people who would not otherwise be using legal services, which helps generate even more business for their firms. Experience shows, the directors say, that if people are referred to a firm and
(35) receive excellent service, the firm will get three to four other referrals who are not plan subscribers and who would therefore pay the firm's standard rate.

But it is unlikely that increased use of such plans will result in long-term client satisfaction or in a
(40) substantial increase in profits for law firms. Since lawyers with established reputations and client bases can benefit little, if at all, from participation, the plans function largely as marketing devices for lawyers who have yet to establish themselves. While
(45) many of these lawyers are no doubt very able and conscientious, they will tend to have less expertise and to provide less satisfaction to clients. At the same time, the downward pressure on fees will mean that the full-fee referrals that proponents say will come
(50) through plan participation may not make up for a

firm's investment in providing services at low plan rates. And since lowered fees provide little incentive for lawyers to devote more than minimal effort to cases, a "volume discount" approach toward the
(55) practice of law will mean less time devoted to complex cases and a general lowering of quality for clients.

1. Which one of the following most accurately expresses the main point of the passage?

(A) In the short term, prepaid legal plans such as the CAW Legal Services Plan appear to be beneficial to both lawyers and clients, but in the long run lawyers will profit at the expense of clients.

(B) The CAW Legal Services Plan and other similar plans represent a controversial, but probably effective, way of bringing down the cost of legal services to clients and increasing lawyers' clientele.

(C) The use of prepaid legal plans such as that of the CAW should be rejected in favor of a more equitable means of making legal services more generally affordable.

(D) In spite of widespread consumer support for legal plans such as that offered by the CAW, lawyers generally criticize such plans, mainly because of their potential financial impact on the legal profession.

(E) Although they have so far attracted many subscribers, it is doubtful whether the CAW Legal Services Plan and other similar prepaid plans will benefit lawyers and clients in the long run.

2. The primary purpose of the passage is to

(A) compare and contrast legal plans with the traditional way of paying for legal services

(B) explain the growing popularity of legal plans

(C) trace the effect of legal plans on prices of legal services

(D) caution that increased use of legal plans is potentially harmful to the legal profession and to clients

(E) advocate reforms to legal plans as presently constituted

GO ON TO THE NEXT PAGE.

3. Which one of the following does the author predict will be a consequence of increased use of legal plans?

 (A) results that are largely at odds with those predicted by lawyers who criticize the plans
 (B) a lowering of the rates such plans charge their members
 (C) forced participation of lawyers who can benefit little from association with the plans
 (D) an eventual increase in profits for lawyers from client usage of the plans
 (E) a reduction in the time lawyers devote to complex cases

4. Which one of the following sequences most accurately and completely corresponds to the presentation of the material in the passage?

 (A) a description of a recently implemented set of procedures and policies; a summary of the results of that implementation; a proposal of refinements in those policies and procedures
 (B) an evaluation of a recent phenomenon; a comparison of that phenomenon with related past phenomena; an expression of the author's approval of that phenomenon
 (C) a presentation of a proposal; a discussion of the prospects for implementing that proposal; a recommendation by the author that the proposal be rejected
 (D) a description of an innovation; a report of reasoning against and reasoning favoring that innovation; argumentation by the author concerning that innovation
 (E) an explanation of a recent occurrence; an evaluation of the practical value of that occurrence; a presentation of further data regarding that occurrence

5. The passage most strongly suggests that, according to proponents of prepaid legal plans, cooperating lawyers benefit from taking clients at lower fees in which one of the following ways?

 (A) Lawyers can expect to gain expertise in a wide variety of legal services by availing themselves of the access to diverse clientele that plan participation affords.
 (B) Experienced cooperating lawyers are likely to enjoy the higher profits of long-term, complex cases, for which new lawyers are not suited.
 (C) Lower rates of profit will be offset by a higher volume of clients and new business through word-of-mouth recommendations.
 (D) Lower fees tend to attract clients away from established, nonparticipating law firms.
 (E) With all legal fees moving downward to match the plans' schedules, the profession will respond to market forces.

6. According to the passage, which one of the following is true of CAW Legal Services Plan members?

 (A) They can enjoy benefits beyond the use of the services of the plan's staff lawyers.
 (B) So far, they generally believe the quality of services they receive from the plan's staff lawyers is as high as that provided by other lawyers.
 (C) Most of them consult lawyers only for relatively simple and routine matters.
 (D) They must pay a fee above the cost of membership for the services of an outside lawyer.
 (E) They do not include only active and retired autoworkers and their families.

7. Which one of the following most accurately represents the primary function of the author's mention of marketing devices (line 43)?

 (A) It points to an aspect of legal plans that the author believes will be detrimental to the quality of legal services.
 (B) It is identified by the author as one of the primary ways in which plan administrators believe themselves to be contributing materially to the legal profession in return for lawyers' participation.
 (C) It identifies what the author considers to be one of the few unequivocal benefits that legal plans can provide.
 (D) It is reported as part of several arguments that the author attributes to established lawyers who oppose plan participation.
 (E) It describes one of the chief burdens of lawyers who have yet to establish themselves and offers an explanation of their advocacy of legal plans.

GO ON TO THE NEXT PAGE.

In the field of historiography—the writing of history based on a critical examination of authentic primary information sources—one area that has recently attracted attention focuses on the responses

(5) of explorers and settlers to new landscapes in order to provide insights into the transformations the landscape itself has undergone as a result of settlement. In this endeavor historiographers examining the history of the Pacific Coast of the

(10) United States have traditionally depended on the records left by European American explorers of the nineteenth century who, as commissioned agents of the U.S. government, were instructed to report thoroughly their findings in writing.

(15) But in furthering this investigation some historiographers have recently recognized the need to expand their definition of what a source is. They maintain that the sources traditionally accepted as documenting the history of the Pacific Coast have too

(20) often omitted the response of Asian settlers to this territory. In part this is due to the dearth of written records left by Asian settlers; in contrast to the commissioned agents, most of the people who first came to western North America from Asia during this

(25) same period did not focus on developing a self-conscious written record of their involvement with the landscape. But because a full study of a culture's historical relationship to its land cannot confine itself to a narrow record of experience, these

(30) historiographers have begun to recognize the value of other kinds of evidence, such as the actions of Asian settlers.

As a case in point, the role of Chinese settlers in expanding agriculture throughout the Pacific Coast

(35) territory is integral to the history of the region. Without access to the better land, Chinese settlers looked for agricultural potential in this generally arid region where other settlers did not. For example, where settlers of European descent looked at willows

(40) and saw only useless, untillable swamp, Chinese settlers saw fresh water, fertile soil, and the potential for bringing water to more arid areas via irrigation. Where other settlers who looked at certain weeds, such as wild mustard, generally saw a nuisance,

(45) Chinese settlers saw abundant raw material for valuable spices from a plant naturally suited to the local soil and climate.

Given their role in the labor force shaping this territory in the nineteenth century, the Chinese settlers

(50) offered more than just a new view of the land. Their vision was reinforced by specialized skills involving swamp reclamation and irrigation systems, which helped lay the foundation for the now well-known and prosperous agribusiness of the region. That

(55) 80 percent of the area's cropland is now irrigated and that the region is currently the top producer of many specialty crops cannot be fully understood by historiographers without attention to the input of Chinese settlers as reconstructed from their

(60) interactions with that landscape.

8. Which one of the following most accurately states the main point of the passage?

(A)   The history of settlement along the Pacific Coast of the U.S., as understood by most historiographers, is confirmed by evidence reconstructed from the actions of Asian settlers.

(B)   Asian settlers on the Pacific Coast of the U.S. left a record of their experiences that traditional historiographers believed to be irrelevant.

(C)   To understand Asian settlers' impact on the history of the Pacific Coast of the U.S., historiographers have had to recognize the value of nontraditional kinds of historiographic evidence.

(D)   Spurred by new findings regarding Asian settlement on the Pacific Coast of the U.S., historiographers have begun to debate the methodological foundations of historiography.

(E)   By examining only written information, historiography as it is traditionally practiced has produced inaccurate historical accounts.

9. Which one of the following most accurately describes the author's primary purpose in discussing Chinese settlers in the third paragraph?

(A)   to suggest that Chinese settlers followed typical settlement patterns in this region during the nineteenth century

(B)   to argue that little written evidence of Chinese settlers' practices survives

(C)   to provide examples illustrating the unique view Asian settlers had of the land

(D)   to demonstrate that the history of settlement in the region has become a point of contention among historiographers

(E)   to claim that the historical record provided by the actions of Asian settlers is inconsistent with history as derived from traditional sources

10. The passage states that the primary traditional historiographic sources of information about the history of the Pacific Coast of the U.S. have which one of the following characteristics?

(A)   They were written both before and after Asian settlers arrived in the area.

(B)   They include accounts by Native Americans in the area.

(C)   They are primarily concerned with potential agricultural uses of the land.

(D)   They focus primarily on the presence of water sources in the region.

(E)   They are accounts left by European American explorers.

GO ON TO THE NEXT PAGE.

11. The author would most likely disagree with which one of the following statements?

   (A) Examining the actions not only of Asian settlers but of other cultural groups of the Pacific Coast of the U.S. is necessary to a full understanding of the impact of settlement on the landscape there.

   (B) The significance of certain actions to the writing of history may be recognized by one group of historiographers but not another.

   (C) Recognizing the actions of Asian settlers adds to but does not complete the writing of the history of the Pacific Coast of the U.S.

   (D) By recognizing as evidence the actions of people, historiographers expand the definition of what a source is.

   (E) The expanded definition of a source will probably not be relevant to studies of regions that have no significant immigration of non-Europeans.

12. According to the passage, each of the following was an aspect of Chinese settlers' initial interactions with the landscape of the Pacific Coast of the U.S. EXCEPT:

   (A) new ideas for utilizing local plants
   (B) a new view of the land
   (C) specialized agricultural skills
   (D) knowledge of agribusiness practices
   (E) knowledge of irrigation systems

13. Which one of the following can most reasonably be inferred from the passage?

   (A) Most Chinese settlers came to the Pacific Coast of the U.S. because the climate was similar to that with which they were familiar.

   (B) Chinese agricultural methods in the nineteenth century included knowledge of swamp reclamation.

   (C) Settlers of European descent used wild mustard seed as a spice.

   (D) Because of the abundance of written sources available, it is not worthwhile to examine the actions of European settlers.

   (E) What written records were left by Asian settlers were neglected and consequently lost to scholarly research.

14. Which one of the following, if true, would most help to strengthen the author's main claim in the last sentence of the passage?

   (A) Market research of agribusinesses owned by descendants of Chinese settlers shows that the market for the region's specialty crops has grown substantially faster than the market for any other crops in the last decade.

   (B) Nineteenth-century surveying records indicate that the lands now cultivated by specialty crop businesses owned by descendants of Chinese settlers were formerly swamp lands.

   (C) Research by university agricultural science departments proves that the formerly arid lands now cultivated by large agribusinesses contain extremely fertile soil when they are sufficiently irrigated.

   (D) A technological history tracing the development of irrigation systems in the region reveals that their efficiency has increased steadily since the nineteenth century.

   (E) Weather records compiled over the previous century demonstrate that the weather patterns in the region are well-suited to growing certain specialty crops as long as they are irrigated.

GO ON TO THE NEXT PAGE.

The survival of nerve cells, as well as their performance of some specialized functions, is regulated by chemicals known as neurotrophic factors, which are produced in the bodies of animals,
(5) including humans. Rita Levi-Montalcini's discovery in the 1950s of the first of these agents, a hormonelike substance now known as NGF, was a crucial development in the history of biochemistry, which led to Levi-Montalcini sharing the Nobel Prize
(10) for medicine in 1986.

In the mid-1940s, Levi-Montalcini had begun by hypothesizing that many of the immature nerve cells produced in the development of an organism are normally programmed to die. In order to confirm this
(15) theory, she conducted research that in 1949 found that, when embryos are in the process of forming their nervous systems, they produce many more nerve cells than are finally required, the number that survives eventually adjusting itself to the volume of
(20) tissue to be supplied with nerves. A further phase of the experimentation, which led to Levi-Montalcini's identification of the substance that controls this process, began with her observation that the development of nerves in chick embryos could be
(25) stimulated by implanting a certain variety of mouse tumor in the embryos. She theorized that a chemical produced by the tumors was responsible for the observed nerve growth. To investigate this hypothesis, she used the then new technique of tissue culture, by
(30) which specific types of body cells can be made to grow outside the organism from which they are derived. Within twenty-four hours, her tissue cultures of chick embryo extracts developed dense halos of nerve tissue near the places in the culture where she
(35) had added the mouse tumor. Further research identified a specific substance contributed by the mouse tumors that was responsible for the effects Levi-Montalcini had observed: a protein that she named "nerve growth factor" (NGF).
(40) NGF was the first of many cell-growth factors to be found in the bodies of animals. Through Levi-Montalcini's work and other subsequent research, it has been determined that this substance is present in many tissues and biological fluids, and that it is
(45) especially concentrated in some organs. In developing organisms, nerve cells apparently receive this growth factor locally from the cells of muscles or other organs to which they will form connections for transmission of nerve impulses, and sometimes from
(50) supporting cells intermingled with the nerve tissue. NGF seems to play two roles, serving initially to direct the developing nerve processes toward the correct, specific "target" cells with which they must connect, and later being necessary for the continued
(55) survival of those nerve cells. During some periods of their development, the types of nerve cells that are affected by NGF—primarily cells outside the brain and spinal cord—die if the factor is not present or if they encounter anti-NGF antibodies.

15. Which one of the following most accurately expresses the main point of the passage?

(A) Levi-Montalcini's discovery of neurotrophic factors as a result of research carried out in the 1940s was a major contribution to our understanding of the role of naturally occurring chemicals, especially NGF, in the development of chick embryos.

(B) Levi-Montalcini's discovery of NGF, a neurotrophic factor that stimulates the development of some types of nerve tissue and whose presence or absence in surrounding cells helps determine whether particular nerve cells will survive, was a pivotal development in biochemistry.

(C) NGF, which is necessary for the survival and proper functioning of nerve cells, was discovered by Levi-Montalcini in a series of experiments using the technique of tissue culture, which she devised in the 1940s.

(D) Partly as a result of Levi-Montalcini's research, it has been found that NGF and other neurotrophic factors are produced only by tissues to which nerves are already connected and that the presence of these factors is necessary for the health and proper functioning of nervous systems.

(E) NGF, a chemical that was discovered by Levi-Montalcini, directs the growth of nerve cells toward the cells with which they must connect and ensures the survival of those nerve cells throughout the life of the organism except when the organism produces anti-NGF antibodies.

16. Based on the passage, the author would be most likely to believe that Levi-Montalcini's discovery of NGF is noteworthy primarily because it

(A) paved the way for more specific knowledge of the processes governing the development of the nervous system

(B) demonstrated that a then new laboratory technique could yield important and unanticipated experimental results

(C) confirmed the hypothesis that many of a developing organism's immature nerve cells are normally programmed to die

(D) indicated that this substance stimulates observable biochemical reactions in the tissues of different species

(E) identified a specific substance, produced by mouse tumors, that can be used to stimulate nerve cell growth

GO ON TO THE NEXT PAGE.

17. The primary function of the third paragraph of the passage in relation to the second paragraph is to

(A) indicate that conclusions referred to in the second paragraph, though essentially correct, require further verification

(B) indicate that conclusions referred to in the second paragraph have been undermined by subsequently obtained evidence

(C) indicate ways in which conclusions referred to in the second paragraph have been further corroborated and refined

(D) describe subsequent discoveries of substances analogous to the substance discussed in the second paragraph

(E) indicate that experimental procedures discussed in the second paragraph have been supplanted by more precise techniques described in the third paragraph

18. Information in the passage most strongly supports which one of the following?

(A) Nerve cells in excess of those that are needed by the organism in which they develop eventually produce anti-NGF antibodies to suppress the effects of NGF.

(B) Nerve cells that grow in the absence of NGF are less numerous than, but qualitatively identical to, those that grow in the presence of NGF.

(C) Few of the nerve cells that connect with target cells toward which NGF directs them are needed by the organism in which they develop.

(D) Some of the nerve cells that grow in the presence of NGF are eventually converted to other types of living tissue by neurotrophic factors.

(E) Some of the nerve cells that grow in an embryo do not connect with any particular target cells.

19. The passage describes a specific experiment that tested which one of the following hypotheses?

(A) A certain kind of mouse tumor produces a chemical that stimulates the growth of nerve cells.

(B) Developing embryos initially grow many more nerve cells than they will eventually require.

(C) In addition to NGF, there are several other important neurotrophic factors regulating cell survival and function.

(D) Certain organs contain NGF in concentrations much higher than in the surrounding tissue.

(E) Certain nerve cells are supplied with NGF by the muscle cells to which they are connected.

20. Which one of the following is most strongly supported by the information in the passage?

(A) Some of the effects that the author describes as occurring in Levi-Montalcini's culture of chick embryo extract were due to neurotrophic factors other than NGF.

(B) Although NGF was the first neurotrophic factor to be identified, some other such factors are now more thoroughly understood.

(C) In her research in the 1940s and 1950s, Levi-Montalcini identified other neurotrophic factors in addition to NGF.

(D) Some neurotrophic factors other than NGF perform functions that are not specifically identified in the passage.

(E) The effects of NGF that Levi-Montalcini noted in her chick embryo experiment are also caused by other neurotrophic factors not discussed in the passage.

GO ON TO THE NEXT PAGE.

The proponents of the Modern Movement in architecture considered that, compared with the historical styles that it replaced, Modernist architecture more accurately reflected the functional
(5) spirit of twentieth-century technology and was better suited to the newest building methods. It is ironic, then, that the Movement fostered an ideology of design that proved to be at odds with the way buildings were really built.

(10) The tenacious adherence of Modernist architects and critics to this ideology was in part responsible for the Movement's decline. Originating in the 1920s as a marginal, almost bohemian art movement, the Modern Movement was never very popular with the public,
(15) but this very lack of popular support produced in Modernist architects a high-minded sense of mission—not content merely to interpret the needs of the client, these architects now sought to persuade, to educate, and, if necessary, to dictate. By 1945 the
(20) tenets of the Movement had come to dominate mainstream architecture, and by the early 1950s, to dominate architectural criticism—architects whose work seemed not to advance the evolution of the Modern Movement tended to be dismissed by
(25) proponents of Modernism. On the other hand, when architects were identified as innovators—as was the case with Otto Wagner, or the young Frank Lloyd Wright—attention was drawn to only those features of their work that were "Modern"; other aspects were
(30) conveniently ignored.

The decline of the Modern Movement later in the twentieth century occurred partly as a result of Modernist architects' ignorance of building methods, and partly because Modernist architects were
(35) reluctant to admit that their concerns were chiefly aesthetic. Moreover, the building industry was evolving in a direction Modernists had not anticipated: it was more specialized and the process of construction was much more fragmented than in
(40) the past. Up until the twentieth century, construction had been carried out by a relatively small number of tradespeople, but as the building industry evolved, buildings came to be built by many specialized subcontractors working independently. The architect's
(45) design not only had to accommodate a sequence of independent operations, but now had to reflect the allowable degree of inaccuracy of the different trades. However, one of the chief construction ideals of the Modern Movement was to "honestly" expose
(50) structural materials such as steel and concrete. To do this and still produce a visually acceptable interior called for an unrealistically high level of craftmanship. Exposure of a building's internal structural elements, if it could be achieved at all,
(55) could only be accomplished at considerable cost—

hence the well-founded reputation of Modern architecture as prohibitively expensive.

As Postmodern architects recognized, the need to expose structural elements imposed unnecessary
(60) limitations on building design. The unwillingness of architects of the Modern Movement to abandon their ideals contributed to the decline of interest in the Modern Movement.

21. Which one of the following most accurately summarizes the main idea of the passage?

(A) The Modern Movement declined because its proponents were overly ideological and did not take into account the facts of building construction.

(B) Rationality was the theoretical basis for the development of the Modern Movement in architecture.

(C) Changes in architectural design introduced by the Modern Movement inspired the development of modern construction methods.

(D) The theoretical bases of the Modern Movement in architecture originated in changes in building construction methods.

(E) Proponents of the Modern Movement in architecture rejected earlier architectural styles because such styles were not functional.

22. Which one of the following is most similar to the relationship described in the passage between the new methods of the building industry and pre-twentieth-century construction?

(A) Clothing produced on an assembly line is less precisely tailored than clothing produced by a single garment maker.

(B) Handwoven fabric is more beautiful than fabric produced by machine.

(C) Lenses ground on a machine are less useful than lenses ground by hand.

(D) Form letters produced by a word processor elicit fewer responses than letters typed individually on a typewriter.

(E) Furniture produced in a factory is less fashionable than handcrafted furniture.

23. With respect to the proponents of the Modern Movement, the author of the passage can best be described as

(A) forbearing
(B) defensive
(C) unimpressed
(D) exasperated
(E) indifferent

GO ON TO THE NEXT PAGE.

24. It can be inferred that the author of the passage believes which one of the following about Modern Movement architects' ideal of exposing structural materials?

   (A) The repudiation of the ideal by some of these architects undermined its validity.
   (B) The ideal was rarely achieved because of its lack of popular appeal.
   (C) The ideal was unrealistic because most builders were unwilling to attempt it.
   (D) The ideal originated in the work of Otto Wagner and Frank Lloyd Wright.
   (E) The ideal arose from aesthetic rather than practical concerns.

25. Which one of the following, in its context in the passage, most clearly reveals the attitude of the author toward the proponents of the Modern Movement?

   (A) "functional spirit" (lines 4–5)
   (B) "tended" (line 24)
   (C) "innovators" (line 26)
   (D) "conveniently" (line 30)
   (E) "degree of inaccuracy" (line 47)

26. The author of the passage mentions Otto Wagner and the young Frank Lloyd Wright (lines 27–28) primarily as examples of

   (A) innovative architects whose work was not immediately appreciated by the public
   (B) architects whom proponents of the Modern Movement claimed represented the movement
   (C) architects whose work helped to popularize the Modern Movement
   (D) architects who generally attempted to interpret the needs of their clients, rather than dictating to them
   (E) architects whose early work seemed to architects of the Modern Movement to be at odds with the principles of Modernism

27. The author of the passage is primarily concerned with

   (A) analyzing the failure of a movement
   (B) predicting the future course of a movement
   (C) correcting a misunderstanding about a movement
   (D) anticipating possible criticism of a movement
   (E) contrasting incompatible viewpoints about a movement

S T O P

IF YOU FINISH BEFORE TIME IS CALLED, YOU MAY CHECK YOUR WORK ON THIS SECTION ONLY.
DO NOT WORK ON ANY OTHER SECTION IN THE TEST.

SECTION II

Time—35 minutes

25 Questions

<u>Directions:</u>   The questions in this section are based on the reasoning contained in brief statements or passages. For some questions, more than one of the choices could conceivably answer the question. However, you are to choose the <u>best</u> answer; that is, the response that most accurately and completely answers the question. You should not make assumptions that are by commonsense standards implausible, superfluous, or incompatible with the passage. After you have chosen the best answer, blacken the corresponding space on your answer sheet.

1. The tidal range at a particular location is the difference in height between high tide and low tide. Tidal studies have shown that one of the greatest tidal ranges in the world is found in the Bay of Fundy and reaches more than seventeen meters. Since the only forces involved in inducing the tides are the sun's and moon's gravity, the magnitudes of tidal ranges also must be explained entirely by gravitational forces.

    Which one of the following most accurately describes a flaw in the reasoning above?

    (A)   It gives only one example of a tidal range.
    (B)   It fails to consider that the size of a tidal range could be affected by the conditions in which gravitational forces act.
    (C)   It does not consider the possibility that low tides are measured in a different way than are high tides.
    (D)   It presumes, without providing warrant, that most activity within the world's oceans is a result of an interplay of gravitational forces.
    (E)   It does not differentiate between the tidal effect of the sun and the tidal effect of the moon.

2. Cardiologist: Coronary bypass surgery is commonly performed on patients suffering from coronary artery disease when certain other therapies would be as effective. Besides being relatively inexpensive, these other therapies pose less risk to the patient since they are less intrusive. Bypass surgery is especially debatable for single-vessel disease.

    The cardiologist's statements, if true, most strongly support which one of the following?

    (A)   Bypass surgery is riskier than all alternative therapies.
    (B)   Needless bypass surgery is more common today than previously.
    (C)   Bypass surgery should be performed when more than one vessel is diseased.
    (D)   Bypass surgery is an especially expensive therapy when used to treat single-vessel disease.
    (E)   Sometimes there are equally effective alternatives to bypass surgery that involve less risk.

3. In the past, combining children of different ages in one classroom was usually a failure; it resulted in confused younger children, who were given inadequate attention and instruction, and bored older ones, who had to sit through previously learned lessons. Recently, however, the practice has been revived with excellent results. Mixed-age classrooms today are stimulating to older children and enable younger children to learn much more efficiently than in standard classrooms.

    Which one of the following, if true, most helps to resolve the apparent discrepancy in the passage?

    (A)   On average, mixed-age classrooms today are somewhat larger in enrollment than were the ones of the past.
    (B)   Mixed-age classrooms of the past were better equipped than are those of today.
    (C)   Today's mixed-age classrooms, unlike those of the past, emphasize group projects that are engaging to students of different ages.
    (D)   Today's mixed-age classrooms have students of a greater range of ages than did those of the past.
    (E)   Few of the teachers who are reviving mixed-age classrooms today were students in mixed-age classrooms when they were young.

GO ON TO THE NEXT PAGE.

4. The top 50 centimeters of soil on Tiliga Island contain bones from the native birds eaten by the islanders since the first human immigration to the island 3,000 years ago. A comparison of this top layer with the underlying 150 centimeters of soil—accumulated over 80,000 years—reveals that before humans arrived on Tiliga, a much larger and more diverse population of birds lived there. Thus, the arrival of humans dramatically decreased the population and diversity of birds on Tiliga.

Which one of the following statements, if true, most seriously weakens the argument?

(A) The bird species known to have been eaten by the islanders had few natural predators on Tiliga.

(B) Many of the bird species that disappeared from Tiliga did not disappear from other, similar, uninhabited islands until much later.

(C) The arrival of a species of microbe, carried by some birds but deadly to many others, immediately preceded the first human immigration to Tiliga.

(D) Bones from bird species known to have been eaten by the islanders were found in the underlying 150 centimeters of soil.

(E) The birds that lived on Tiliga prior to the first human immigration generally did not fly well.

5. The corpus callosum—the thick band of nerve fibers connecting the brain's two hemispheres—of a musician is on average larger than that of a nonmusician. The differences in the size of corpora callosa are particularly striking when adult musicians who began training around the age of seven are compared to adult nonmusicians. Therefore, musical training, particularly when it begins at a young age, causes certain anatomic brain changes.

Which one of the following is an assumption on which the argument depends?

(A) The corpora callosa of musicians, before they started training, do not tend to be larger than those of nonmusicians of the same age.

(B) Musical training late in life does not cause anatomic changes to the brain.

(C) For any two musicians whose training began around the age of seven, their corpora callosa are approximately the same size.

(D) All musicians have larger corpora callosa than do any nonmusicians.

(E) Adult nonmusicians did not participate in activities when they were children that would have stimulated any growth of the corpus callosum.

6. Chai: The use of the word "tree" to denote both deciduous and coniferous plant forms, while acceptable as a lay term, is scientifically inadequate; it masks the fact that the two plant types have utterly different lineages.

Dodd: But the common name highlights the crucial fact that both are composed of the same material and have very similar structures; so it is acceptable as a scientific term.

The conversation provides the strongest grounds for holding that Chai and Dodd disagree over whether

(A) it is advisable to use ordinary terms as names for biological forms in scientific discourse

(B) using the same term for two biological forms with different lineages can be scientifically acceptable

(C) both deciduous and coniferous plant forms evolved from simpler biological forms

(D) it is important that the lay terms for plant forms reflect the current scientific theories about them

(E) biological forms with similar structures can have different lineages

7. Increases in the occurrence of hearing loss among teenagers are due in part to their listening to loud music through stereo headphones. So a group of concerned parents is recommending that headphone manufacturers include in their product lines stereo headphones that automatically turn off when a dangerous level of loudness is reached. It is clear that adoption of this recommendation would not significantly reduce the occurrence of hearing loss in teenagers, however, since almost all stereo headphones that teenagers use are bought by the teenagers themselves.

Which one of the following, if true, provides the most support for the argument?

(A) Loud music is most dangerous to hearing when it is played through stereo headphones.

(B) No other cause of hearing loss in teenagers is as damaging as their listening to loud music through stereo headphones.

(C) Parents of teenagers generally do not themselves listen to loud music through stereo headphones.

(D) Teenagers who now listen to music at dangerously loud levels choose to do so despite their awareness of the risks involved.

(E) A few headphone manufacturers already plan to market stereo headphones that automatically turn off when a dangerous level of loudness is reached.

8. Most plants have developed chemical defenses against parasites. The average plant contains about 40 natural pesticides—chemical compounds toxic to bacteria, fungi, and other parasites. Humans ingest these natural pesticides without harm every day. Therefore, the additional threat posed by synthetic pesticides sprayed on crop plants by humans is minimal.

    Each of the following, if true, weakens the argument EXCEPT:

    (A)   Humans have been consuming natural plant pesticides for millennia and have had time to adapt to them.
    (B)   The concentrations of natural pesticides in plants are typically much lower than the concentrations of synthetic pesticides in sprayed crop plants.
    (C)   Natural plant pesticides are typically less potent than synthetic pesticides, whose toxicity is highly concentrated.
    (D)   Natural plant pesticides generally serve only as defenses against specific parasites, whereas synthetic pesticides are often harmful to a wide variety of organisms.
    (E)   The synthetic pesticides sprayed on crop plants by humans usually have chemical structures similar to those of the natural pesticides produced by the plants.

9. In addition to the labor and materials used to make wine, the reputation of the vineyard where the grapes originate plays a role in determining the price of the finished wine. Therefore, an expensive wine is not always a good wine.

    Which one of the following is an assumption on which the argument depends?

    (A)   The price of a bottle of wine should be a reflection of the wine's quality.
    (B)   Price is never an accurate indication of the quality of a bottle of wine.
    (C)   The reputation of a vineyard does not always indicate the quality of its wines.
    (D)   The reputation of a vineyard generally plays a greater role than the quality of its grapes in determining its wines' prices.
    (E)   Wines produced by lesser-known vineyards generally are priced to reflect accurately the wines' quality.

10. Before their larvae hatch, each parental pair of *Nicrophorus* beetles buries the carcass of a small vertebrate nearby. For several days after the larvae hatch, both beetles feed their voracious larvae from the carcass, which is entirely consumed within a week. Since both parents help with feeding, larvae should benefit from both parents' presence; however, removing one parent before the hatching results in larvae that grow both larger and heavier than they otherwise would be.

    Which one of the following, if true, best helps to explain why removing one parent resulted in larger, heavier larvae?

    (A)   Two beetles can find and bury a larger carcass than can a single beetle.
    (B)   Both parents use the carcass as their own food supply for as long as they stay with the larvae.
    (C)   Beetle parents usually take turns feeding their larvae, so that there is always one provider available and one at rest.
    (D)   After a week, the larvae are capable of finding other sources of food and feeding themselves.
    (E)   Two parents can defend the carcass from attack by other insects better than a single parent can.

11. For many centuries it was believed that only classical Euclidean geometry could provide a correct way of mathematically representing the universe. Nevertheless, scientists have come to believe that a representation of the universe employing non-Euclidean geometry is much more useful in developing certain areas of scientific theory. In fact, such a representation underlies the cosmological theory that is now most widely accepted by scientists as accurate.

    Which one of the following is most strongly supported by the statements above?

    (A)   Scientists who use Euclidean geometry are likely to believe that progress in mathematical theory results in progress in natural science.
    (B)   Scientists generally do not now believe that classical Euclidean geometry is uniquely capable of giving a correct mathematical representation of the universe.
    (C)   Non-Euclidean geometry is a more complete way of representing the universe than is Euclidean geometry.
    (D)   An accurate scientific theory cannot be developed without the discovery of a uniquely correct way of mathematically representing the universe.
    (E)   The usefulness of a mathematical theory is now considered by scientists to be more important than its mathematical correctness.

GO ON TO THE NEXT PAGE.

12. Experts hired to testify in court need to know how to make convincing presentations. Such experts are evaluated by juries in terms of their ability to present the steps by which they arrived at their conclusions clearly and confidently. As a result, some less expert authorities who are skilled at producing convincing testimony are asked to testify rather than highly knowledgeable but less persuasive experts.

Which one of the following most closely conforms to the principle illustrated by the passage above?

(A) Successful politicians are not always the ones who best understand how to help their country. Some lack insight into important political issues but are highly skilled at conducting an election campaign.

(B) Trial lawyers often use the techniques employed by actors to influence the emotions of jurors. Many lawyers have studied drama expressly for the purpose of improving their courtroom skills.

(C) The opera singer with the best voice is the appropriate choice even for minor roles, despite the fact that an audience may be more affected by a singer with greater dramatic ability but a lesser voice.

(D) It is often best to try to train children with gentle reinforcement of desired behavior, rather than by simply telling them what to do and what not to do. This results in children who behave because they want to, not because they feel compelled.

(E) Job applicants are usually hired because their skills and training best meet a recognized set of qualifications. Only rarely is a prospective employer convinced to tailor a position to suit the skills of a particular applicant.

13. The solution to any environmental problem that is not the result of government mismanagement can only lie in major changes in consumer habits. But major changes in consumer habits will occur only if such changes are economically enticing. As a result, few serious ecological problems will be solved unless the solutions are made economically enticing.

The conclusion drawn in the argument above follows logically if which one of the following is assumed?

(A) Few serious ecological problems are the result of government mismanagement.

(B) No environmental problems that stem from government mismanagement have solutions that are economically feasible.

(C) Major changes in consumer habits can be made economically enticing.

(D) Most environmental problems that are not the result of government mismanagement are major ecological problems.

(E) Few serious ecological problems can be solved by major changes in consumer habits.

14. The economy is doing badly. First, the real estate slump has been with us for some time. Second, car sales are at their lowest in years. Of course, had either one or the other phenomenon failed to occur, this would be consistent with the economy as a whole being healthy. But, their occurrence together makes it quite probable that my conclusion is correct.

Which one of the following inferences is most strongly supported by the information above?

(A) If car sales are at their lowest in years, then it is likely that the economy is doing badly.

(B) If the economy is doing badly, then either the real estate market or the car sales market is not healthy.

(C) If the real estate market is healthy, then it is likely that the economy as a whole is healthy.

(D) If the economy is in a healthy state, then it is unlikely that the real estate and car sales markets are both in a slump.

(E) The bad condition of the economy implies that both the real estate and the car sales markets are doing badly.

GO ON TO THE NEXT PAGE.

15. According to current geological theory, the melting of ice at the end of the Ice Age significantly reduced the weight pressing on parts of the earth's crust. As a result, lasting cracks in the earth's crust appeared in some of those parts under the stress of pressure from below. At the end of the Ice Age Sweden was racked by severe earthquakes. Therefore, it is likely that the melting of the ice contributed to these earthquakes.

Which one of the following, if true, most strengthens the argument above?

(A)   The earth's crust tends to crack whenever there is a sudden change in the pressures affecting it.

(B)   There are various areas in Northern Europe that show cracks in the earth's crust.

(C)   Evidence of severe earthquakes around the time of the end of the Ice Age can be found in parts of northern Canada.

(D)   Severe earthquakes are generally caused by cracking of the earth's crust near the earthquake site.

(E)   Asteroid impacts, which did occur at the end of the Ice Age, generally cause severe earthquakes.

16. Sociologist: Some economists hold that unregulated markets should accompany democratic sovereignty because they let people vote with their money. But this view ignores the crucial distinction between the private consumer and the public citizen. In the marketplace the question is, "What do I want?" At the voting booth the question is always, "What do we want?" Hence, supporters of political democracy can also support marketplace regulation.

Which one of the following most accurately expresses the conclusion drawn by the sociologist?

(A)   Voters think of themselves as members of a community, rather than as isolated individuals.

(B)   Unregulated markets are incompatible with democratic sovereignty.

(C)   Where there is democratic sovereignty there should be unregulated markets.

(D)   Private consumers are primarily concerned with their own self-interest.

(E)   Opposition to unregulated markets is consistent with support for democracy.

17. The tiny hummingbird weighs little, but its egg is 15 percent of the adult hummingbird's weight. The volume and weight of an adult goose are much greater than those of a hummingbird, but a goose's egg is only about 4 percent of its own weight. An adult ostrich, much larger and heavier than a goose, lays an egg that is only 1.6 percent of its own weight.

Which one of the following propositions is best illustrated by the statements above?

(A)   The eggs of different bird species vary widely in their ratio of volume to weight.

(B)   The smaller and lighter the average adult members of a bird species are, the larger and heavier the eggs of that species are.

(C)   The ratio of egg weight of a species to body weight of an adult member of that species is smaller for larger birds than for smaller ones.

(D)   The size of birds' eggs varies greatly from species to species but has little effect on the volume and weight of the adult bird.

(E)   Bird species vary more in egg size than they do in average body size and weight.

18. Bram Stoker's 1897 novel *Dracula* portrayed vampires—the "undead" who roam at night to suck the blood of living people—as able to turn into bats. As a result of the pervasive influence of this novel, many people now assume that a vampire's being able to turn into a bat is an essential part of vampire myths. However, this assumption is false, for vampire myths existed in Europe long before Stoker's book.

Which one of the following is an assumption on which the argument depends?

(A)   At least one of the European vampire myths that predated Stoker's book did not portray vampires as strictly nocturnal.

(B)   Vampire myths in Central and South America, where real vampire bats are found, portray vampires as able to turn into bats.

(C)   Vampire myths did not exist outside Europe before the publication of Stoker's *Dracula*.

(D)   At least one of the European vampire myths that predated Stoker's book did not portray vampires as able to turn into bats.

(E)   At the time he wrote *Dracula*, Stoker was familiar with earlier European vampire myths.

GO ON TO THE NEXT PAGE.

19. It is unlikely that the world will ever be free of disease. Most diseases are caused by very prolific microorganisms whose response to the pressures medicines exert on them is predictable: they quickly evolve immunities to those medicines while maintaining their power to infect and even kill humans.

Which one of the following most accurately describes the role played in the argument by the claim that it is unlikely that the world will ever be free of disease?

(A) It is a conclusion that is claimed to follow from the premise that microorganisms are too numerous for medicines to eliminate entirely.

(B) It is a conclusion for which a description of the responses of microorganisms to the medicines designed to cure the diseases they cause is offered as support.

(C) It is a premise offered in support of the claim that most disease-causing microorganisms are able to evolve immunities to medicines while retaining their ability to infect humans.

(D) It is a generalization used to predict the response of microorganisms to the medicines humans use to kill them.

(E) It is a conclusion that is claimed to follow from the premise that most microorganisms are immune to medicines designed to kill them.

20. Scientist: My research indicates that children who engage in impulsive behavior similar to adult thrill-seeking behavior are twice as likely as other children to have a gene variant that increases sensitivity to dopamine. From this, I conclude that there is a causal relationship between this gene variant and an inclination toward thrill-seeking behavior.

Which one of the following, if true, most calls into question the scientist's argument?

(A) Many impulsive adults are not unusually sensitive to dopamine.

(B) It is not possible to reliably distinguish impulsive behavior from other behavior.

(C) Children are often described by adults as engaging in thrill-seeking behavior simply because they act impulsively.

(D) Many people exhibit behavioral tendencies as adults that they did not exhibit as children.

(E) The gene variant studied by the scientist is correlated with other types of behavior in addition to thrill-seeking behavior.

21. It is highly likely that Claudette is a classical pianist. Like most classical pianists, Claudette recognizes many of Clara Schumann's works. The vast majority of people who are not classical pianists do not. In fact, many people who are not classical pianists have not even heard of Clara Schumann.

The reasoning in the argument above is flawed in that it

(A) ignores the possibility that Claudette is more familiar with the works of other composers of music for piano

(B) presumes, without providing justification, that people who have not heard of Clara Schumann do not recognize her works

(C) presumes, without providing justification, that classical pianists cannot also play other musical instruments

(D) relies for its plausibility on the vagueness of the term "classical"

(E) ignores the possibility that the majority of people who recognize many of Clara Schumann's works are not classical pianists

GO ON TO THE NEXT PAGE.

22. All the evidence so far gathered fits both Dr. Grippen's theory and Professor Heissmann's. However, the predictions that these theories make about the result of the planned experiment cannot both be true. Therefore, the result of this experiment will confirm one of these theories at the expense of the other.

The argument above exhibits an erroneous pattern of reasoning most similar to that exhibited by which one of the following?

(A)   David and Jane both think they know how to distinguish beech trees from elms, but when they look at trees together they often disagree. Therefore, at least one of them must have an erroneous method.

(B)   Although David thinks the tree they saw was a beech, Jane thinks it was an elm. Jane's description of the tree's features is consistent with her opinion, so this description must be inconsistent with David's view.

(C)   David and Jane have been equally good at identifying trees so far. But David says this one is an elm, whereas Jane is unsure. Therefore, if this tree turns out to be an elm, we'll know David is better.

(D)   David thinks that there are more beeches than elms in this forest. Jane thinks he is wrong. The section of forest we examined was small, but examination of the whole forest would either confirm David's view or disprove it.

(E)   David thinks this tree is a beech. Jane thinks it is an elm. Maria, unlike David or Jane, is expert at tree identification, so when Maria gives her opinion it will verify either David's or Jane's opinion.

23. Columnist: The relief from the drudgery of physical labor that much modern technology affords its users renders them dependent on this technology, and, more importantly, on the elaborate energy systems required to run it. This leads to a loss of self-sufficiency. Clearly, then, in addition to undermining life's charm, much modern technology diminishes the overall well-being of its users.

Which one of the following is an assumption required by the columnist's argument?

(A)   Physical labor is essential to a fulfilling life.
(B)   Self-sufficiency contributes to a person's well-being.
(C)   People are not free if they must depend on anything other than their own capacities.
(D)   Anything causing a loss in life's charm is unjustifiable unless this loss is compensated by some gain.
(E)   Technology inherently limits the well-being of its users.

GO ON TO THE NEXT PAGE.

24. Psychologist: Some psychologists mistakenly argue that because dreams result from electrical discharges in the brain, they must be understood purely in terms of their physiological function. They conclude, against Freud, that dreams reveal nothing about the character of the dreamer. But since dream content varies enormously, then even if electrical discharges provide the terms of the physiological explanation of dreams, they cannot completely explain the phenomenon of dreaming.

The claim that dream content varies enormously plays which one of the following roles in the argument?

(A) It is used to support the anti-Freudian conclusion that some psychologists draw concerning dreams.

(B) It is used to support the explicitly stated conclusion that a fully satisfactory account of dreams must allow for the possibility of their revealing significant information about the dreamer.

(C) It is used to suggest that neither Freud's theory nor the theory of anti-Freudian psychologists can completely explain the phenomenon of dreaming.

(D) It is used to illustrate the difficulty of providing a complete explanation of the phenomenon of dreaming.

(E) It is used to undermine a claim that some psychologists use to argue against a view of Freud's.

25. The first bicycle, the Draisienne, was invented in 1817. A brief fad ensued, after which bicycles practically disappeared until the 1860s. Why was this? New technology is accepted only when it coheres with the values of a society. Hence some change in values must have occurred between 1817 and the 1860s.

The reasoning in the argument is flawed because the argument

(A) presumes, without giving justification, that fads are never indicative of genuine acceptance

(B) fails to recognize that the reappearance of bicycles in the 1860s may have indicated genuine acceptance of them

(C) offers no support for the claim that the Draisienne was the first true bicycle

(D) poses a question that has little relevance to the argument's conclusion

(E) ignores, without giving justification, alternative possible explanations of the initial failure of bicycles

S T O P

IF YOU FINISH BEFORE TIME IS CALLED, YOU MAY CHECK YOUR WORK ON THIS SECTION ONLY.
DO NOT WORK ON ANY OTHER SECTION IN THE TEST.

SECTION III

Time—35 minutes

22 Questions

Directions: Each group of questions in this section is based on a set of conditions. In answering some of the questions, it may be useful to draw a rough diagram. Choose the response that most accurately and completely answers each question and blacken the corresponding space on your answer sheet.

Questions 1–6

In the course of one month Garibaldi has exactly seven different meetings. Each of her meetings is with exactly one of five foreign dignitaries: Fuentes, Matsuba, Rhee, Soleimani, or Tbahi. The following constraints govern Garibaldi's meetings:

> She has exactly three meetings with Fuentes, and exactly one with each of the other dignitaries.
> She does not have any meetings in a row with Fuentes.
> Her meeting with Soleimani is the very next one after her meeting with Tbahi.
> Neither the first nor last of her meetings is with Matsuba.

1. Which one of the following could be the sequence of the meetings Garibaldi has with the dignitaries?

   (A) Fuentes, Rhee, Tbahi, Soleimani, Fuentes, Matsuba, Rhee
   (B) Fuentes, Tbahi, Soleimani, Matsuba, Fuentes, Fuentes, Rhee
   (C) Fuentes, Rhee, Fuentes, Matsuba, Fuentes, Tbahi, Soleimani
   (D) Fuentes, Tbahi, Matsuba, Fuentes, Soleimani, Rhee, Fuentes
   (E) Fuentes, Tbahi, Soleimani, Fuentes, Rhee, Fuentes, Matsuba

2. If Garibaldi's last meeting is with Rhee, then which one of the following could be true?

   (A) Garibaldi's second meeting is with Soleimani.
   (B) Garibaldi's third meeting is with Matsuba.
   (C) Garibaldi's fourth meeting is with Soleimani.
   (D) Garibaldi's fifth meeting is with Matsuba.
   (E) Garibaldi's sixth meeting is with Soleimani.

3. If Garibaldi's second meeting is with Fuentes, then which one of the following is a complete and accurate list of the dignitaries with any one of whom Garibaldi's fourth meeting could be?

   (A) Fuentes, Soleimani, Rhee
   (B) Matsuba, Rhee, Tbahi
   (C) Matsuba, Soleimani
   (D) Rhee, Tbahi
   (E) Fuentes, Soleimani

4. If Garibaldi's meeting with Rhee is the very next one after Garibaldi's meeting with Soleimani, then which one of the following must be true?

   (A) Garibaldi's third meeting is with Fuentes.
   (B) Garibaldi's fourth meeting is with Rhee.
   (C) Garibaldi's fifth meeting is with Fuentes.
   (D) Garibaldi's sixth meeting is with Rhee.
   (E) Garibaldi's seventh meeting is with Fuentes.

5. If Garibaldi's first meeting is with Tbahi, then Garibaldi's meeting with Rhee could be the

   (A) second meeting
   (B) third meeting
   (C) fifth meeting
   (D) sixth meeting
   (E) seventh meeting

6. If Garibaldi's meeting with Matsuba is the very next meeting after Garibaldi's meeting with Rhee, then with which one of the following dignitaries must Garibaldi's fourth meeting be?

   (A) Fuentes
   (B) Matsuba
   (C) Rhee
   (D) Soleimani
   (E) Tbahi

GO ON TO THE NEXT PAGE.

Questions 7–12

During a certain week, an animal shelter places exactly six dogs—a greyhound, a husky, a keeshond, a Labrador retriever, a poodle, and a schnauzer—with new owners. Two are placed on Monday, two on Tuesday, and the remaining two on Wednesday, consistent with the following conditions:

The Labrador retriever is placed on the same day as the poodle.

The greyhound is not placed on the same day as the husky.

If the keeshond is placed on Monday, the greyhound is placed on Tuesday.

If the schnauzer is placed on Wednesday, the husky is placed on Tuesday.

7. Which one of the following could be a complete and accurate matching of dogs to the days on which they are placed?

(A)   Monday: greyhound, Labrador retriever
         Tuesday: husky, poodle
         Wednesday: keeshond, schnauzer
(B)   Monday: greyhound, keeshond
         Tuesday: Labrador retriever, poodle
         Wednesday: husky, schnauzer
(C)   Monday: keeshond, schnauzer
         Tuesday: greyhound, husky
         Wednesday: Labrador retriever, poodle
(D)   Monday: Labrador retriever, poodle
         Tuesday: greyhound, keeshond
         Wednesday: husky, schnauzer
(E)   Monday: Labrador retriever, poodle
         Tuesday: husky, keeshond
         Wednesday: greyhound, schnauzer

8. Which one of the following must be true?

(A)   The keeshond is not placed on the same day as the greyhound.
(B)   The keeshond is not placed on the same day as the schnauzer.
(C)   The schnauzer is not placed on the same day as the husky.
(D)   The greyhound is placed on the same day as the schnauzer.
(E)   The husky is placed on the same day as the keeshond.

9. If the poodle is placed on Tuesday, then which one of the following could be true?

(A)   The greyhound is placed on Monday.
(B)   The keeshond is placed on Monday.
(C)   The Labrador retriever is placed on Monday.
(D)   The husky is placed on Tuesday.
(E)   The schnauzer is placed on Wednesday.

10. If the greyhound is placed on the same day as the keeshond, then which one of the following must be true?

(A)   The husky is placed on Monday.
(B)   The Labrador retriever is placed on Monday.
(C)   The keeshond is placed on Tuesday.
(D)   The poodle is not placed on Wednesday.
(E)   The schnauzer is not placed on Wednesday.

11. If the husky is placed the day before the schnauzer, then which one of the following CANNOT be true?

(A)   The husky is placed on Monday.
(B)   The keeshond is placed on Monday.
(C)   The greyhound is placed on Tuesday.
(D)   The poodle is placed on Tuesday.
(E)   The poodle is placed on Wednesday.

12. If the greyhound is placed the day before the poodle, then which one of the following CANNOT be placed on Tuesday?

(A)   the husky
(B)   the keeshond
(C)   the Labrador retriever
(D)   the poodle
(E)   the schnauzer

GO ON TO THE NEXT PAGE.

Questions 13–17

A tour group plans to visit exactly five archaeological sites. Each site was discovered by exactly one of the following archaeologists—Ferrara, Gallagher, Oliphant—and each dates from the eighth, ninth, or tenth century (A.D.). The tour must satisfy the following conditions:

The site visited second dates from the ninth century.
Neither the site visited fourth nor the site visited fifth was discovered by Oliphant.
Exactly one of the sites was discovered by Gallagher, and it dates from the tenth century.
If a site dates from the eighth century, it was discovered by Oliphant.
The site visited third dates from a more recent century than does either the site visited first or that visited fourth.

13. Which one of the following could be an accurate list of the discoverers of the five sites, listed in the order in which the sites are visited?

(A) Oliphant, Oliphant, Gallagher, Oliphant, Ferrara
(B) Gallagher, Oliphant, Ferrara, Ferrara, Ferrara
(C) Oliphant, Gallagher, Oliphant, Ferrara, Ferrara
(D) Oliphant, Oliphant, Gallagher, Ferrara, Gallagher
(E) Ferrara, Oliphant, Gallagher, Ferrara, Ferrara

14. If exactly one of the five sites the tour group visits dates from the tenth century, then which one of the following CANNOT be a site that was discovered by Ferrara?

(A) the site visited first
(B) the site visited second
(C) the site visited third
(D) the site visited fourth
(E) the site visited fifth

15. Which one of the following could be a site that dates from the eighth century?

(A) the site visited first
(B) the site visited second
(C) the site visited third
(D) the site visited fourth
(E) the site visited fifth

16. Which one of the following is a complete and accurate list of the sites each of which CANNOT be the site discovered by Gallagher?

(A) third, fourth, fifth
(B) second, third, fourth
(C) first, fourth, fifth
(D) first, second, fifth
(E) first, second, fourth

17. The tour group could visit at most how many sites that were discovered by Ferrara?

(A) one
(B) two
(C) three
(D) four
(E) five

GO ON TO THE NEXT PAGE.

Questions 18–22

Each day of a five-day workweek (Monday through Friday), Anastasia parks for the entire day in exactly one of three downtown parking lots—X, Y, and Z. One of the lots costs $10 for the day, another costs $12, and the other costs $15. Anastasia parks in each of the three lots at least once during her workweek. The following conditions must apply:

On Thursday, Anastasia parks in the $15 lot.

Lot X costs more than lot Z.

The lot Anastasia parks in on Wednesday costs more than the one she parks in on Friday.

Anastasia parks in lot Z on more days of the workweek than she parks in lot X.

18. Which one of the following could be a complete and accurate list of which lot Anastasia parks in each day, listed in order from Monday through Friday?

(A) Y, Z, X, Y, Z
(B) Y, Z, Z, Y, X
(C) Z, Z, X, X, Y
(D) Z, Z, X, X, Z
(E) Z, Z, X, Z, Y

19. Anastasia CANNOT park in the $15 lot on which one of the following days?

(A) Monday
(B) Tuesday
(C) Wednesday
(D) Thursday
(E) Friday

20. If lot Z is the $12 lot, then on which one of the following days must Anastasia park in lot Y?

(A) Monday
(B) Tuesday
(C) Wednesday
(D) Thursday
(E) Friday

21. Anastasia CANNOT park in lot Z on which one of the following days?

(A) Monday
(B) Tuesday
(C) Wednesday
(D) Thursday
(E) Friday

22. Which one of the following could be a complete and accurate list of the days on which Anastasia parks in the $10 lot?

(A) Monday
(B) Tuesday
(C) Monday, Tuesday
(D) Monday, Wednesday
(E) Monday, Thursday

S T O P

IF YOU FINISH BEFORE TIME IS CALLED, YOU MAY CHECK YOUR WORK ON THIS SECTION ONLY.
DO NOT WORK ON ANY OTHER SECTION IN THE TEST.

SECTION IV
Time—35 minutes
26 Questions

<u>Directions:</u> The questions in this section are based on the reasoning contained in brief statements or passages. For some questions, more than one of the choices could conceivably answer the question. However, you are to choose the <u>best</u> answer; that is, the response that most accurately and completely answers the question. You should not make assumptions that are by commonsense standards implausible, superfluous, or incompatible with the passage. After you have chosen the best answer, blacken the corresponding space on your answer sheet.

1. Jones fell unconscious on the job and it was suspected that he had swallowed a certain chemical, so he was rushed to the local hospital's emergency room. In making her diagnosis, the emergency-room physician knew that if Jones had swallowed the chemical, a deficiency in the content of a mineral in his blood would result. She also knew that deficiency in the mineral causes inflammation of the skin. Since Jones's skin was not inflamed when he was admitted to the emergency room, the physician concluded that Jones had not swallowed the chemical.

   Which one of the following, if true, would undermine the physician's conclusion?

   (A) Jones did not know that the chemical was dangerous.
   (B) Jones had suffered inflammation of the skin in the past.
   (C) It takes 48 hours for the chemical to bring about deficiency of the mineral in the blood.
   (D) Jones often worked with the chemical.
   (E) Deficiency in minerals other than the mineral in question can cause inflammation of the skin.

2. Pacifist: It is immoral to do anything that causes harm to another person. But, since using force causes harm to another person, it is also immoral to threaten to use force, even when such a threat is made in self-defense.

   Which one of the following principles, if valid, would most help to justify the pacifist's reasoning?

   (A) Given the potential harm caused by the use of force, the line between use of force in self-defense and the aggressive use of force is always vague.
   (B) It is immoral to threaten to do what it is immoral to do.
   (C) It is immoral to do anything that causes more harm than good.
   (D) Whether a threat made in self-defense is immoral depends on the circumstances.
   (E) It is immoral to carry out a threat if making the threat is itself immoral.

3. Beginning in the 1950s, popular music was revolutionized by the electrification of musical instruments, which has enabled musicians to play with increased volume. Because individual musicians can play with increased volume, the average number of musicians per band has decreased. Nevertheless, electrification has increased rather than decreased the overall number of musicians who play popular music professionally.

   Which one of the following is most strongly supported by the statements above, if those statements are true?

   (A) The number of amateur musicians who play popular music has decreased.
   (B) Most professional musicians are able to play both electric and nonelectric instruments.
   (C) The number of professional musicians in some bands has increased.
   (D) The total number of professional bands has increased as a result of electrification.
   (E) Many professional musicians play in more than one band.

4. Statistics indicating a sudden increase in the incidence of a problem often merely reflect a heightened awareness of the problem or a greater ability to record its occurrence. Hence we should be wary of proposals for radical solutions to problems when those proposals are a reaction to new statistical data.

   The argumentation conforms most closely to which one of the following principles?

   (A) A better cognizance of a problem does not warrant the undertaking of a radical solution to the problem.
   (B) Attempts to stop the occurrence of a problem should be preceded by a determination that the problem actually exists.
   (C) Proposals for radical solutions to problems should be based on statistical data alone.
   (D) Statistical data should not be manipulated to make a radical solution to a problem seem more justified than it actually is.
   (E) Radical solutions to problems can cause other problems and end up doing more harm than good.

GO ON TO THE NEXT PAGE.

5. Barr: The National Tea Association cites tea's recent visibility in advertising and magazine articles as evidence of tea's increasing popularity. However, a neutral polling company, the Survey Group, has tracked tea sales at numerous stores for the last 20 years and has found no change in the amount of tea sold. We can thus conclude that tea is no more popular now than it ever was.

Which one of the following, if true, most seriously weakens Barr's argument?

(A) The National Tea Association has announced that it plans to carry out its own retail survey in the next year.

(B) A survey by an unrelated polling organization shows that the public is generally receptive to the idea of trying new types of tea.

(C) The Survey Group is funded by a consortium of consumer advocacy groups.

(D) The stores from which the Survey Group collected information about tea sales are all located in the same small region of the country.

(E) Tea has been the subject of an expensive and efficient advertising campaign funded, in part, by the National Tea Association.

6. Doctors urge people to reduce their cholesterol levels through dietary changes. But moderate dietary changes often do not work to lower cholesterol levels. One may need, therefore, to make more dramatic changes, such as switching to a vegetarian diet.

The statement that moderate dietary changes often do not work to lower cholesterol levels plays which one of the following roles in the argument?

(A) It is presented to counter doctors' suggestions that cholesterol levels can be reduced through dietary changes.

(B) It is a premise offered in support of the claim that vegetarian diets are more healthful than any diets containing meat.

(C) It is a premise offered in support of the claim that reducing cholesterol levels may require greater than moderate dietary changes.

(D) It is offered as an explanation of the success of vegetarian diets in reducing cholesterol levels.

(E) It is a conclusion for which the claim that dramatic changes in one's diet are sometimes required to reduce cholesterol levels is offered as support.

7. Since empathy is essential for people to be willing to follow moral codes that sometimes require them to ignore their own welfare to help others, civilized society could not exist without empathy.

Which one of the following is an assumption required by the argument?

(A) Civilized society can exist only if there are people who are willing to at least sometimes ignore their own welfare to help others.

(B) Failure to empathize with other people usually leads to actions detrimental to civilized society.

(C) If everyone in a society is sometimes willing to ignore his or her own welfare to help others, that society will be civilized.

(D) Moral codes that include the requirement that people disregard their own welfare in order to help others have arisen within some civilized societies.

(E) People who feel empathy tend to ignore their own welfare for the sake of others.

8. Insurgent political parties that are profoundly dissatisfied with the dominant party's reign and justificatory ideology always produce factions whose views and aims differ as greatly from each other's as they do from the dominant party's. Although these factions ignore their own disagreements for the sake of defeating the dominant party, their disagreements inevitably come forward upon victory. Therefore, _____.

Which one of the following is the most logical completion of the argument?

(A) no victorious insurgent party ever manages to stay in power for as long as the party it displaces did

(B) a victorious insurgent party must address the disagreements between its factions if it is to stay in power

(C) the heretofore insurgent party will not always promulgate a new ideology to justify its own policies, once it is victorious

(D) a victorious insurgent party always faces opposition from the party it recently ousted

(E) it is impossible for the different factions of a victorious insurgent party to effect the compromises necessary to keep the new party in power

GO ON TO THE NEXT PAGE.

9. Manager: When Sullivan was passed over for promotion, people said that the deciding factor was his being much older than the competition. But this is clearly not the case. Several recent promotions have been given to people older than Sullivan.

    The manager's argument is most vulnerable to criticism because it fails to consider the possibility that

    (A) Sullivan was well qualified for the promotion
    (B) age is only one of a number of factors that kept Sullivan from being promoted
    (C) people often associate age with experience and good judgment
    (D) the people older than Sullivan who were promoted had no younger competitors
    (E) Sullivan's employer tries to keep deliberations involving promotion decisions confidential

10. Council member P: Alarmists are those who see an instance of pollution and exaggerate its significance into a major character fault of society. Such alarmists fail to distinguish the incident and the behavior that caused it from the disposition of people not to pollute.

    Council member Q: To think that there is a lot of pollution based on the discovery of a serious single instance of pollution is simply an application of the widely accepted principle that actions tend to follow the path of least resistance, and it is surely easier to pollute than not to pollute.

    Council members P and Q disagree over whether

    (A) pollution should be considered a problem
    (B) actions tend to follow the path of least resistance
    (C) people are responsible for pollution
    (D) people can change their behavior and not pollute
    (E) people are inclined to pollute

11. It is easy to see that the board of directors of the construction company is full of corruption and should be replaced. There are many instances of bribery by various persons on the staff of board member Wagston that are a matter of public record. These bribes perniciously influenced the awarding of government contracts.

    The argument's reasoning is most vulnerable to criticism on the grounds that

    (A) the argument fails to show that corruption is not limited to Wagston's staff
    (B) the argument fails to show that Wagston's staff engaged in any bribery other than bribery of government officials
    (C) the argument fails to specify the relation between bribery and corruption
    (D) the argument presumes without giving justification that all of Wagston's staff have engaged in corruption
    (E) the argument attempts to deflect attention away from substantive issues by attacking the character of the board

12. Coffee and tea contain methylxanthines, which cause temporary increases in the natural production of vasopressin, a hormone produced by the pituitary gland. Vasopressin causes clumping of blood cells, and the clumping is more pronounced in women than in men. This is probably the explanation of the fact that women face as much as a tenfold higher risk than men do of complications following angioplasty, a technique used to clear clogged arteries.

    Which one of the following statements is most strongly supported by the information above?

    (A) Men, but not women, should be given methylxanthines prior to undergoing angioplasty.
    (B) In spite of the risks, angioplasty is the only effective treatment for clogged arteries.
    (C) Women probably drink more coffee and tea, on average, than do men.
    (D) Prior to undergoing angioplasty, women should avoid coffee and tea.
    (E) Angioplasty should not be used to treat clogged arteries.

GO ON TO THE NEXT PAGE.

13. Whether a machine performs its intended function is plain for all to see, but recognition of excellence in art requires a rare subtlety of perception. So whereas engineers usually maintain their composure when their work is being evaluated, artists tend to become anxious under such circumstances.

The reasoning above conforms most closely to which one of the following propositions?

(A) People who have an interest in working as artists are no more likely to have especially anxious personalities than are people who have an interest in working as engineers.

(B) The value of a machine is independent of the feelings of those who create it, while the value of an artwork is not.

(C) Evaluation of the work of engineers should be based on a different set of standards than is evaluation of the work of artists.

(D) People who create things whose success can be easily ascertained worry less about others' opinions of their work than do people who create things whose value cannot be easily ascertained.

(E) Someone who creates a work that cannot be easily evaluated tends to be less confident about its value than are those who evaluate it.

14. Scientists hypothesize that a particular type of fat known as "P-fat" is required for the development of eyesight. Researchers were led to this hypothesis by observing that babies who are fed formulas low in P-fat tend to have worse eyesight than babies fed mother's milk, which is high in P-fat. It has also been shown that babies that are five to six weeks premature tend to have worse eyesight than babies carried to term.

Which one of the following, if true, most supports the scientists' hypothesis?

(A) Adults whose diets lack P-fat tend to have worse eyesight than those whose diets are high in P-fat.

(B) A fetus typically receives high levels of P-fat from the mother during only the last four weeks of pregnancy.

(C) Babies whose mothers have poor eyesight do not tend to have poor eyesight themselves.

(D) Babies generally prefer mother's milk to formulas low in P-fat.

(E) The eyesight of a fetus develops during the last trimester of pregnancy.

15. Artists have different ways of producing contours and hatching, and analysis of these stylistic features can help to distinguish works by a famous artist both from forgeries and from works genuinely by other artists. Indeed, this analysis has shown that many of the drawings formerly attributed to Michelangelo are actually by the artist Giulio Clovio, Michelangelo's contemporary.

If the statements above are true, then which one of the following must also be true?

(A) Contours and hatching are the main features that distinguish the drawing styles of different artists.

(B) Many of the drawings formerly attributed to Michelangelo are actually forgeries.

(C) No forgery can perfectly duplicate the contour and hatching styles of a famous artist.

(D) The contour and hatching styles used to identify the drawings of Clovio cited can be shown to be features of all Clovio's works.

(E) There is an analyzable difference between Clovio's contour and hatching styles and those of Michelangelo.

16. Moralist: Immoral actions are those that harm other people. But since such actions eventually harm those who perform them, those who act immorally do so only through ignorance of some of their actions' consequences rather than through a character defect.

Which one of the following is an assumption required by the moralist's argument?

(A) People ignorant of their actions' consequences cannot be held morally responsible for those consequences.

(B) An action harms those who perform it only if it also eventually harms others.

(C) Only someone with a character defect would knowingly perform actions that eventually harm others.

(D) Those who, in acting immorally, eventually harm themselves do not intend that harm.

(E) None of those who knowingly harm themselves lack character defects.

GO ON TO THE NEXT PAGE.

17. Climatologists believe they know why Earth has undergone a regular sequence of ice ages beginning around 800,000 years ago. Calculations show that Earth's orbit around the Sun has fluctuations that coincide with the ice-age cycles. The climatologists hypothesize that when the fluctuations occur, Earth passes through clouds of cosmic dust that enters the atmosphere; the cosmic dust thereby dims the Sun, resulting in an ice age. They concede, however, that though cosmic dust clouds are common, the clouds would have to be particularly dense in order to have this effect.

Each of the following, if true, would lend support to the climatologists' hypothesis EXCEPT:

(A) Earth did not pass through clouds of cosmic dust earlier than 800,000 years ago.

(B) Two large asteroids collided 800,000 years ago, producing a tremendous amount of dense cosmic dust that continues to orbit the Sun.

(C) Earth's average temperature drops slightly shortly after volcanic eruptions spew large amounts of dust into Earth's atmosphere.

(D) Large bits of cosmic rock periodically enter Earth's atmosphere, raising large amounts of dust from Earth's surface.

(E) Rare trace elements known to be prevalent in cosmic debris have been discovered in layers of sediment whose ages correspond very closely to the occurrence of ice ages.

18. Philosopher: The rational pursuit of happiness is quite different from always doing what one most strongly desires to do. This is because the rational pursuit of happiness must include consideration of long-term consequences, whereas our desires are usually focused on the short term. Moreover, desires are sometimes compulsions, and while ordinary desires result in at least momentary happiness when their goals are attained, compulsions strongly drive a person to pursue goals that offer no happiness even when reached.

If all of the philosopher's statements are true, each of the following could be true EXCEPT:

(A) The majority of people do not have compulsions.

(B) Attaining the goal of any desire results in momentary happiness.

(C) Most people do not pursue happiness rationally.

(D) Most people want more than their own personal happiness.

(E) All actions have long-term consequences.

19. Political scientist: All governments worthy of respect allow their citizens to dissent from governmental policies. No government worthy of respect leaves minorities unprotected. Thus any government that protects minorities permits criticism of its policies.

The flawed pattern of reasoning in which one of the following most closely parallels that in the political scientist's argument?

(A) Politicians are admirable if they put the interests of those they serve above their own interests. So politicians who sometimes ignore the interests of their own constituents in favor of the nation as a whole deserve admiration, for they are putting the interests of those they serve above their own.

(B) All jazz musicians are capable of improvising and no jazz musician is incapable of reading music. Therefore all musicians who can read music can improvise.

(C) Ecosystems with cool, dry climates are populated by large mammals. No ecosystems populated by large mammals have abundant and varied plant life. Thus ecosystems that do not have cool, dry climates have abundant and varied plant life.

(D) Some intellectuals are not socially active, and no intellectual is a professional athlete. Therefore any professional athlete is socially active.

(E) First-person narratives reveal the thoughts of the narrator but conceal those of the other characters. Some third-person narratives reveal the motives of every character. Thus books that rely on making all characters' motives apparent should be written in the third person.

GO ON TO THE NEXT PAGE.

20. Advertisement: Each of the Economic Merit Prize winners from the past 25 years is covered by the Acme retirement plan. Since the winners of the nation's most prestigious award for economists have thus clearly recognized that the Acme plan offers them a financially secure future, it is probably a good plan for anyone with retirement needs similar to theirs.

The advertisement's argumentation is most vulnerable to criticism on which one of the following grounds?

(A) It ignores the possibility that the majority of Economic Merit Prize winners from previous years used a retirement plan other than the Acme plan.

(B) It fails to address adequately the possibility that any of several retirement plans would be good enough for, and offer a financially secure future to, Economic Merit Prize winners.

(C) It appeals to the fact that supposed experts have endorsed the argument's main conclusion, rather than appealing to direct evidence for that conclusion.

(D) It takes for granted that some winners of the Economic Merit Prize have deliberately selected the Acme retirement plan, rather than having had it chosen for them by their employers.

(E) It presumes, without providing justification, that each of the Economic Merit Prize winners has retirement plan needs that are identical to the advertisement's intended audience's retirement plan needs.

21. A small car offers less protection in an accident than a large car does, but since a smaller car is more maneuverable, it is better to drive a small car because then accidents will be less likely.

Which one of the following arguments employs reasoning most similar to that employed by the argument above?

(A) An artist's best work is generally that done in the time before the artist becomes very well known. When artists grow famous and are diverted from artistic creation by demands for public appearances, their artistic work suffers. So artists' achieving great fame can diminish their artistic reputations.

(B) It is best to insist that a child spend at least some time every day reading indoors. Even though it may cause the child some unhappiness to have to stay indoors when others are outside playing, the child can benefit from the time by learning to enjoy books and becoming prepared for lifelong learning.

(C) For this work, vehicles built of lightweight materials are more practical than vehicles built of heavy materials. This is so because while lighter vehicles do not last as long as heavier vehicles, they are cheaper to replace.

(D) Although it is important to limit the amount of sugar and fat in one's diet, it would be a mistake to try to follow a diet totally lacking in sugar and fat. It is better to consume sugar and fat in moderation, for then the cravings that lead to uncontrolled binges will be prevented.

(E) A person who exercises vigorously every day has less body fat than an average person to draw upon in the event of a wasting illness. But one should still endeavor to exercise vigorously every day, because doing so significantly decreases the chances of contracting a wasting illness.

GO ON TO THE NEXT PAGE.

22. Trainer: Research shows that when dogs are neutered in early puppyhood, their leg bones usually do not develop properly. Improper bone development leads in turn to problems with arthritis as dogs grow older. Thus, if you want to protect your dog from arthritis you should not neuter your dog until it is full-grown.

Of the following, which one is a criticism to which the reasoning in the trainer's argument is most vulnerable?

(A) It fails to state exactly what percentage of dogs neutered in early puppyhood experience improper bone development.
(B) It fails to explain the connection between improper bone development and arthritis.
(C) It fails to address the effects of neutering in middle or late puppyhood.
(D) It fails to consider the possibility that the benefits of neutering a dog early might outweigh the risk of arthritis.
(E) It fails to consider the possibility that dogs with properly developed bones can develop arthritis.

23. Political scientist: One of the most interesting dilemmas in contemporary democratic politics concerns the regulation of political campaign spending. People certainly should be free, within broad limits, to spend their money as they choose. On the other hand, candidates who can vastly outspend all rivals have an unfair advantage in publicizing their platforms. Democratic governments have a strong obligation to ensure that all voices have an equal chance to be heard, but governments should not subsidize expensive campaigns for each candidate. The resolution of the dilemma, therefore, is clear: _____.

Which one of the following most logically completes the political scientist's argument?

(A) only candidates with significant campaign resources should be permitted to run for public office
(B) an upper limit on the political campaign spending of each candidate is warranted
(C) government subsidization of all political campaigns at a low percentage of their total cost is warranted
(D) all wealthy persons should be prohibited from spending their own money on political campaigns
(E) each candidate should be allowed to spend as much money on a political campaign as any other candidate chooses to spend

24. Some people have maintained that private ownership of the means of production ultimately destroys any society that sanctions it. This may be true of a less technologically advanced society that must share its economic resources to survive. But since only private ownership of the means of production permits individuals to test new technologies without the majority's consent, a technologically advanced society will actually endanger its survival if the means of production become public property.

The proposition that private ownership of the means of production ultimately destroys any society that sanctions it plays which one of the following roles in the argument above?

(A) It is a generalization that the argument suggests is no more applicable to less technologically advanced societies than to more technologically advanced societies.
(B) It is a hypothesis for whose widespread acceptance the argument offers an explanation.
(C) It is a general hypothesis that the argument suggests is inapplicable to societies more dependent for survival upon the introduction of new technologies than upon the sharing of resources.
(D) It is a contention about the consequences of an economic arrangement that the argument claims is incompatible with the needs of any society.
(E) It is a generalization about societies that according to the argument is true for any society in which the majority of its citizens does not impede the introduction of new technologies.

GO ON TO THE NEXT PAGE.

25. A certain medication that is frequently prescribed to lower a patient's cholesterol level is generally effective. A recent study of 1,000 subjects ranging widely in age indicates, however, that the cholesterol level of someone taking the medication is typically 12 to 15 percent higher than the average for that person's age group.

Which one of the following, if true, most helps to explain how both of the claims made above could be true?

(A) A recently developed cholesterol-lowering medication is more effective than the medication described above.

(B) Another medication is prescribed to treat high cholesterol just as often as the medication described above is.

(C) In most cases, people with high cholesterol levels are not treated with drug therapy but are put on restrictive low-cholesterol diets.

(D) The medication described above is usually prescribed only for people whose cholesterol level is at least 30 percent above the average for their age group.

(E) Within the population as a whole, approximately the same number of people have relatively high cholesterol levels as have relatively low cholesterol levels.

26. Political theorist: For all of its members to be strong in foreign policy, an alliance of countries must respond aggressively to problems. An alliance will do so only if every member of the alliance perceives the problems as grave. But the European Union countries will not all perceive a problem as grave unless they all agree that it threatens their alliance's economy. Thus, not all of the member countries of the European Union will be strong in foreign policy.

The conclusion drawn above follows logically if which one of the following is assumed?

(A) Countries that refuse to join alliances generally respond more aggressively to problems than do countries that do join alliances.

(B) Countries become less aggressive in foreign policy if greater wealth leads them to think that they have more to lose by responding to problems aggressively.

(C) Problems that appear to some member countries of the European Union to threaten the alliance's economy will not appear so to others.

(D) European Union member countries that fail to perceive the economic relevance of problems are generally weak in foreign policy.

(E) Alliances that are economically beneficial for a given country are not necessarily beneficial with regard to foreign policy.

S T O P

IF YOU FINISH BEFORE TIME IS CALLED, YOU MAY CHECK YOUR WORK ON THIS SECTION ONLY.
DO NOT WORK ON ANY OTHER SECTION IN THE TEST.

Acknowledgment is made to the following sources from which material has been adapted for use in this test booklet:

Marsha Kideckel, "Pre-Paid Legal Plans: Legal Help for Less or Less Help?" ©October 1989 by Canadian Lawyer.

Patty Limerick, "American Landscape Discovered from the West." ©1992 by the Journal of American History.

LSAT® Writing Sample Topic

The program manager of a public television station intends to purchase a documentary program on diabetes and has narrowed the choice down to two programs. Write an argument for purchasing one program over the other, taking into account the following:

- The program manager wants to increase youth awareness of diabetes by engaging a younger audience.
- The program manager wants to air a well-researched and accurate depiction of the challenges of living with diabetes.

"What's Up, Doc?" tells the story of 19-year-old Carlene, a popular rap artist. A physician who worked with Carlene is interviewed, but the documentary focuses primarily on Carlene, her family, and the musicians who work with her. The discussion centers on how Carlene has dealt with her diabetes since it was diagnosed at the age of 14. Carlene explains the innovative and interesting ways she found to integrate the daily monitoring and control of the disease into her very demanding schedule. The program touches on risk factors, warning signs, complications, and self-care skills for managing diabetes. Carlene ends the program by directing a plea to teenagers to learn about the symptoms of diabetes and become more aware of the disease.

"Living with Diabetes" is an investigation of teenagers with diabetes in four different high schools across the country narrated by Andre Smith, a well-known, prizewinning health reporter. Smith interviews a number of students with the disease, along with school administrators and teachers, about the effect of diabetes on the students' lives. He visits local hospitals and counseling centers to interview doctors and psychologists, who outline the various physical and psychological effects of diabetes. The camera also takes viewers to the Diabetes Research Institute's information outreach program, where visitors meet researchers and learn what they are doing to find a cure for the disease. Included in the program are detailed descriptions of treatment options available and their costs, as well as advice about prevention and testing.

WP-L024-A

Scratch Paper
Do not write your essay in this space.

Directions:

1. Use the Answer Key on the next page to check your answers.

2. Use the Scoring Worksheet below to compute your raw score.

3. Use the Score Conversion Chart to convert your raw score into the 120-180 scale.

Scoring Worksheet

1. Enter the number of questions you answered correctly in each section.

                                    Number
                                    Correct

   SECTION I. . . . . . _____
   SECTION II . . . . . _____
   SECTION III. . . . . _____
   SECTION IV. . . . . _____

2. Enter the sum here: _____
                          This is your Raw Score.

Conversion Chart
For Converting Raw Score to the 120-180 LSAT Scaled Score
LSAT Form G-4LSN61

Reported Score	Raw Score Lowest	Raw Score Highest
180	98	100
179	—*	—*
178	97	97
177	96	96
176	95	95
175	—*	—*
174	94	94
173	93	93
172	92	92
171	91	91
170	90	90
169	89	89
168	88	88
167	87	87
166	85	86
165	84	84
164	82	83
163	81	81
162	80	80
161	78	79
160	76	77
159	75	75
158	73	74
157	72	72
156	70	71
155	68	69
154	67	67
153	65	66
152	63	64
151	61	62
150	60	60
149	58	59
148	56	57
147	54	55
146	53	53
145	51	52
144	49	50
143	47	48
142	46	46
141	44	45
140	42	43
139	41	41
138	39	40
137	37	38
136	36	36
135	34	35
134	32	33
133	31	31
132	29	30
131	28	28
130	26	27
129	25	25
128	23	24
127	22	22
126	20	21
125	19	19
124	17	18
123	16	16
122	15	15
121	14	14
120	0	13

*There is no raw score that will produce this scaled score for this form.

SECTION I

1.	E	8.	C	15.	B	22.	A
2.	D	9.	C	16.	A	23.	C
3.	E	10.	E	17.	C	24.	E
4.	D	11.	E	18.	E	25.	D
5.	C	12.	D	19.	A	26.	B
6.	A	13.	B	20.	D	27.	A
7.	A	14.	B	21.	A		

SECTION II

1.	B	8.	E	15.	D	22.	E
2.	E	9.	C	16.	E	23.	B
3.	C	10.	B	17.	C	24.	E
4.	C	11.	B	18.	D	25.	E
5.	A	12.	A	19.	B		
6.	B	13.	A	20.	B		
7.	D	14.	D	21.	E		

SECTION III

1.	C	8.	B	15.	A	22.	C
2.	D	9.	A	16.	E		
3.	E	10.	E	17.	D		
4.	E	11.	D	18.	A		
5.	D	12.	A	19.	E		
6.	A	13.	E	20.	E		
7.	E	14.	C	21.	D		

SECTION IV

1.	C	8.	B	15.	E	22.	C
2.	B	9.	D	16.	D	23.	B
3.	D	10.	E	17.	D	24.	C
4.	A	11.	A	18.	B	25.	D
5.	D	12.	A	19.	B	26.	C
6.	C	13.	D	20.	D		
7.	A	14.	B	21.	E		

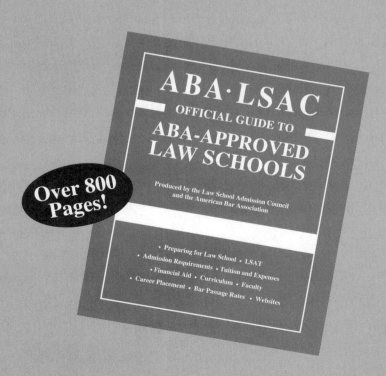

visit us at:

www.LSAC.org
Quick, convenient, and
secure online services!

- *Register for the LSAT*

- *Register for the LSDAS*

- *Process your letters of recommendation*

- *Check the status of your LSAC file and electronic law school applications*

- *Order LSAT prep materials, videos, software, and publications*

- *Apply to law schools electronically*

- *Search for the right law school at no charge using the ABA-LSAC Official Guide to ABA-Approved Law Schools online edition*

- *Download a free, previously administered LSAT*

- *Check service updates, changing news, and much MORE!*